MW00856675

the Entertaining Touch

DEDICATION
For all those who love to bring life to the party.

Copyright © 2006 by Hoffman Media, LLC
Publishers of *Southern Lady* Magazine

All rights reserved. No part of this book may be reproduced or transmitted in any form or by any means, electronic or mechanical, including photocopying, or by any information storage and retrieval system, without permission in writing from Hoffman Media, LLC. Reviewers may quote brief passages for specific inclusion in a magazine or newspaper.

First published in 2006 by Hoffman Media, LLC.
Birmingham, Alabama
With offices at:
1900 International Park Drive, Suite 50
Birmingham, Alabama 35243
www.hoffmanmedia.com

ISBN # 0978548957

Publisher Phyllis Hoffman

Editor Andrea Fanning

Style Director Yukie McLean

Creative Director Mac Jamieson

Art Director Jordan Marxer

Test Kitchen Director Rebecca Touliatos

Food Editor Aimee Bishop

Production Director Greg Baugh

Color Technician Delisa McDaniel

Copy Editor Ann Dorer

Written by Andrea Fanning with
Karen Dauphin and Lauren Rippey

Photography by Mac Jamieson,
Marcy Black, and Arden Ward

the Entertaining Touch

RECIPES AND INSPIRATION FOR EVERY OCCASION

A publication of *Southern Lady* Magazine

Hoffman Media, LLC

Birmingham, Alabama

Contents

Introduction

There is a moment just before your guests arrive when all is ready to receive them. The linens are pressed. The crystal sparkles. The silver shines. Like a beautifully wrapped present, this gathering is your gift to those you love. Soon, the doorbell rings and the giving begins as you share with each guest your uniquely wonderful entertaining touch.

Throughout our lives, the memories we make are colored by the settings and surroundings we experience. The sweet scent of blossoming lilies, the rich taste of delectable peach Melba, the lovely sight of friendly and familiar faces—so vividly do we recall the details and delights of group gatherings around a beautiful table.

Here in the South, we are always searching for reasons to bring together the ones we love. And in this book, you'll find lots of ideas for good-time gatherings: a porch party to welcome fall, an open house to meet new neighbors, a flower swap to kick-off the garden club's summer meetings.

Such occasions give us opportunities to shine. Whether it is a hand-inscribed place card or a delicious batch of shortbread cookies, the smallest gestures—what we at *Southern Lady* call "entertaining touches"—can turn an ordinary assembly into something extra special. In fact, this entire book is designed to give you ideas and inspiration for ways to host your own memory-making events.

From beginning to end, *The Entertaining Touch* includes both the foundation and information you need to host most any kind of party. You'll find helpful hints and tips as well as creative ideas for everything from flower arranging to table setting.

A particular color scheme may catch your eye, or maybe you'll discover a theme that piques your curiosity. You may choose a china pattern similar to one that is featured or even decide to recreate an identical design. Perhaps you'll try a recipe or two from here and there, or maybe you'll prepare an entire menu, a feat that is certain to please.

No matter how you choose to use this compilation, our hope is that these pages will offer you a picturesque escape into a world of Southern style. It is our sincerest wish that these words and photographs will tickle your fancy, delight your eyes, and tempt your tastebuds. But most of all, we seek to provide a source of inspiration and delight to you, the reader. So, come. Be our guest, and enjoy this, a journey into the enchantment of entertaining.

—Andrea Fanning, editor

the Entertaining essentials

No matter what kind of party you are hosting, a few basic principles apply. Certainly, good food is a staple at any gathering—especially a Southern one—and you'll find that this book is filled with an abundance of recipes and menu ideas with which to delight your guests and their tastebuds. The themes you use to design your events are important, too, along with the confidence that comes from following simple rules of modern etiquette.

Though protocol has changed over the years and continues to evolve, the philosophy of hospitality remains the same. As host or hostess, you want to make your guests feel welcomed and comfortable. Whenever you're in doubt about party particulars, use this goal as your guide. In addition to this general rule, however, be sure to heed our entertaining essentials, items of note that all potential party planners should know.

The next few pages focus on the basic preparations for entertaining. Where does the white wine glass go in the place setting? How many forks should be on the table at any given time? How do you word a casual dinner invitation? What does R.S.V.P. stand for? You'll find the answers to these questions and many more as you explore the general guidelines pertinent to today's hosts and hostesses.

STERLING SERVICE

Guests are coming—what joy! Happy preparations ready the sparklling setting for a most memorable day of entertaining and celebration.

From familiar varieties of forks, knives, and spoons to serving pieces like tongs, trays, and ladles, tools of the hostessing trade are steeped in tradition. Once carried in small pouches attached at the belt, flatware is now set aside as cherished family heirlooms and highly prized collectibles. That is, until a party is planned, and it's time to polish your pretties. Rather than viewing the care of silver as a chore, consider it a time to lovingly tend to exquisite treasures. Relax and reminisce, allowing your mind to drift to all the happy occasions where these precious pieces have graced convivial meals shared by friends and loved ones.

- Clean silver flatware and serving accessories as soon after use as possible.

- Store silver correctly in airtight silverware chests or tarnish-resistant cloth bags.

- Keep silver out of direct sunlight, avoid dampness, and never wrap or bind with plastic or foil.

- To polish, first rinse in hot water to remove surface dust, then apply silver cream quickly with a moistened sponge. Wash with a mild dishwashing liquid, rinse with warm water, then dry with a soft cotton cloth, buffing gently until silver gleams.

- Silver may be polished up to three weeks in advance, which can save precious minutes during party preparations.

SETTING THE TABLE

"Ponder well on this point: The pleasant hours of our life are all connected, by a more or less intangible link, with some memory of the table."

—*Charles Pierre Monselet*

Whether you're planning an intimate dinner for two or a celebration for two dozen, your table sets the tone for the entire occasion. Embrace the challenge and dazzle fellow diners with the most pristine of place settings.

Begin with your tablecloth—the foundation of your table. More formal dinners suggest traditional white clothes, but solid colors and lace are perfectly acceptable. If you do choose a patterned cloth, make sure it does not compete with your attention-worthy china.

Next up is dinnerware. From casual ceramics to classic china, a multitude of styles can enliven your party's personality, making quite an impact on the overall tablescape. Choose a standard setting, or mix and match shapes and colors from different collections. Don't be afraid to be creative; remember, as host or hostess, this is your time to shine!

Once you've selected the perfect plates and bowls, accessorize with cutlery, china, and glasses (see page 14). Forks go on the left, knives and spoons on the right, all in order of use, from the outside in. Turn your knife blades toward the plate and place bread plates to the left. If you have just one glass, place it at the tip of the dinner knife. More than one glass? Arrange them in order of use, beginning with the outermost one.

From there, napkins add a punch of pizzazz to an already-sparkling table. Typically placed to the left of plates, napkins with the prettiest of rings (see page 24) and the fanciest of folds (see page 26) deserve a front-and-center spot directly on the dinner plate.

Last, but certainly not least, place cards ensure everyone feels like a guest of honor. Traditionally in the form of black calligraphy on white, modern hosts often choose to mirror the mood of the party with mini pumpkins at Thanksgiving or ornaments at Christmastime. Use your imagination and seat guests in such a fashion that will allow them to mix and mingle, encouraging the flow of conversation and guaranteeing the grandest of times.

Begin your perfect table setting by placing chargers one inch from the edge of the table. Then, align flatware handles with the bottom rim of the dinner plate, making sure pieces are evenly spaced.

SETTING A *Formal Table*

When it comes to a formal table, remember that the key is to present the setting in a way that will not intimidate your guests. You should always cater the setting to match the various courses of the particular meal. If you are serving a fish course or shrimp appetizer, you will need to add the appropriate flatware. As a general rule, no more than three knives, three forks, and a spoon are initially laid on the table. Known as the Rule of Three, this suggestion helps prevent a cluttered table. If additional utensils are required, they should be brought out with their respective dishes. Stemware should be limited to four glasses per person. If desired, dessert wine and coffee may be served individually as the meal progresses.

A Salad Plate

B Napkin

C Salad Fork

D Dinner Fork

E Dinner Plate

F Dinner Knife

G Spoon

H Bread Plate

I Bread Knife

J Dessert Spoon

K Dessert Fork

L Water Goblet

M Red Wine

N White Wine

Designed for everyday use, the casual setting features basic dinnerware, glassware, and serving utensils. Since this style is more familiar, some may find the task of setting a formal table a bit daunting, but it helps to remember that both follow the same basic format. The dinner plate—with or without a charger—should be centered in front of the guest's seat. Generally, forks are placed to the left of the plate, and knives and spoons to the right. Once that is done, the setting should simply suit the occasion and the menu.

SETTING A
Casual Table

A Salad Plate	E Dinner Plate	I Bread Knife
B Napkin	F Dinner Knife	J Water Goblet
C Salad Fork	G Spoon	K Iced Tea Glass
D Dinner Fork	H Bread Plate	

INVITATION SENSATIONS

R.S.V.P. stands for the French phrase *repondez s'il vous plait,* which means "reply, please." Including this on an invitation encourages those invited to respond whether or not they plan to attend the event and aids the hostess in making preparations.

The first impression guests have when you plan an event is the invitation that you send. Successful invites should match the occasion in style and formality, provide all the necessary information, and also capture the interest of the invited person, who will hopefully view your party as a "can't miss" event.

Traditionally, the formal invitation is engraved on a white or ecru card in black ink. Other formal options include the engraved fill-in—often used by those who host dinner parties quite frequently—or a version of personal stationery. Useful for a variety occasions, the informal invitation offers much more flexibility and variation in terms of style, paper, color, wording, and creativity.

Regardless of which type of invitation you use for an event, it should include all the pertinent information: the name(s) of the host(s), the purpose of the invitation, the location of the event, and its day, date, and time. On formal invitations, spell out both the day and time. If it is necessary to note appropriate attire, do so. For planning purposes, it is also best to include R.S.V.P. (or R.s.v.p.) information so you will have an estimate of how many guests will attend.

Invitations should be extended at least three to six weeks prior to the date of the event. If it is an especially big occasion or one that occurs at a busy social season such as the Christmas holidays, send invitations at least six to eight weeks in advance. To help your guests plan accordingly for a large event, you may want to send "save the date" cards several months prior. Remember to follow up with those who have not responded; any number of reasons could have prevented their reply, and you want to make sure they have received the invitation.

EXAMPLES OF *Invitations*

Mr. and Mrs. Jamie Hodges
request the pleasure of your company
at Dinner
on Saturday, the fifth of March
at eight o'clock
726 Somerset Avenue

R.S.V.P
726 Somerset Avenue
Nashville, TN 37203

FORMAL

Please join us for dinner
on Friday, October 21st
at 7:30 p.m.
417 Bryant Drive

R.S.V.P.
Jody & Erica Dodd
722-2000

INFORMAL

Join us for dinner on the beach Saturday, June 3rd at 6:00 pm

327 Beach Road
Orange Beach, Alabama

Hosted by:
Taylor and Tiffany Robb
RSVP by Friday, May 26th
to 334-555-0000

Please join us to celebrate the
Holiday Season
with good friends, and good cheer

Come And Help Paint
Tristan's Dining Room!

We'll learn great painting techniques and faux
finishes...plus enjoy lots of good food!

Sunday, May 8th at 2:00 pm

Come And Help Paint
Tristan's Dining Room!

We'll learn great painting techniques and faux
finishes...plus enjoy lots of good food!

Sunday, May 8th at 2:00 pm

Please join us for
A Plant Swap Luncheon!
Saturday, the thirteenth of May
at eleven o'cl

Laura Barring

128 Brookwood Ro

Birmingham, Ala

Please bring a plant t

Inviting Ideas

Create invitations with the occasion's theme in mind. Most
of the materials you'll need are available at your local
craft or scrapbook supply store. CLOCKWISE FROM TOP
LEFT: Turn paint swatches—available for free at your local
home improvement store—into a clever way to enliven
the anticipation for an upcoming painting party (see page
36). A short length of striped ribbon adds a lovely touch
to a monogrammed invitation to the garden club's flower
swap (see page 76). Tucked inside an embossed envelope,
a handwritten note attached to sheet music covered with
floral-embellished vellum sets the tone for a romantic
dinner and candlelight serenade (see page 156). OPPOSITE:
Delicate gold wire and beautiful beads elegantly adorn an
invitation to a glittering holiday gathering (see page 174).

Darling,
Please join me
for a very special
dinner tonight.
Love, Tiffany

the *Entertaining extras*

The difference between a simply average event and one thought to be absolutely sensational is found in the details. To host one of these incredible affairs requires that you reach beyond the expected and into the realm of creativity.

Ideas can spring from practically anywhere, but if you find yourself in need of assistance, simply delve into this chapter for a little inspiration. Remembering that your main objective revolves around treating your guests to a pleasant experience, you should always seek ways to make those in attendance feel special.

A beautiful tablescape gives you an excellent starting point. Once the place settings have been positioned, you can concentrate on adding those extra touches that will complete your table's dazzling transformation. An eclectic mix of heirloom napkin rings, a lovely piece of jewelry-turned-table ornament, a patterned napkin folded into the shape of an envelope—just imagine the possibilities.

Instead of storing unused serving pieces and silver away, polish and display them prominently in the room as clever conversation starters. Thoughtfully combine plates from different china patterns to add interest as well as unique beauty. By including a few enchanting embellishments, such as fresh-cut flowers and selections from an antique collection, you'll see that a little bit of effort will go a long way in achieving a look that's not only inviting, but also a tangible illustration of your personal touch.

Perhaps the following pages will ignite a creative spark in you, so be ready and willing to try your hand at some or all of the projects awaiting your perusal. Even better, you may find that the flames of innovation and imagination have begun to burn fast and bright as you consider various interpretations and adaptations to fit your own entertaining endeavors.

Look to your favorite collections to find inspiration for adding a personal touch to your party planning.

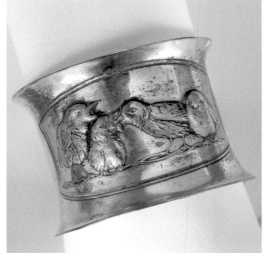

DAZZLING DETAILS

Rings and Things

With just the tiniest of touches, you can add decorative flair to any table setting. CLOCKWISE FROM TOP LEFT: A store-bought napkin ring becomes a new type of finishing touch when placed in the center of a uniquely trimmed napkin folded into a flower shape. Bracelets and brooches from the jewelry box and even a fancy hairclip bring glamour to the table when fashioned as napkin rings. A ruby and amythest tassel lends beaded elegance to a pretty place setting. OPPOSITE: A single blossom and small grapevine wreath—painted white—come together to present an elegant complement to white linens. To avoid pollen stains on the fabric, first cut off the pollen-loaded tips of the flower's stamen.

THE ART OF NAPKIN FOLDING

the envelope

Quarter Fold: This basic step is often used in napkin folding. Start with a napkin laid flat. Fold in half lengthwise by bringing the bottom long edge up to the top. Press with an iron. Fold in half again, bringing the left side over to the right to create a small square. Press.

Step 1. Complete Quarter Fold. With the open corners at the top, fold the left and right points to the center and press. Fold the point of the bottom corner up over these two corners.

Step 2. Fold top flap down over the center of the square, overlapping like an envelope. For an added touch, use a monogrammed napkin.

the pretty pocket

Step 1. Start with a napkin laid flat on its back. Bring the bottom edge of the napkin up two-thirds of the way and fold flat. Press.

Step 2. Bring the top one-third of the napkin down over the lower fold, meeting the bottom edge of the rectangle. Rotate so the napkin opens to the top. Press.

Step 3. Fold the top flap down so its edge lies 1½ inches from the bottom edge of the rectangle. Press.

Step 4. Flip the napkin over so folds are on the back. Bring the left and right ends in, meeting at the center. Press.

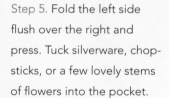

Step 5. Fold the left side flush over the right and press. Tuck silverware, chopsticks, or a few lovely stems of flowers into the pocket.

crowning touch

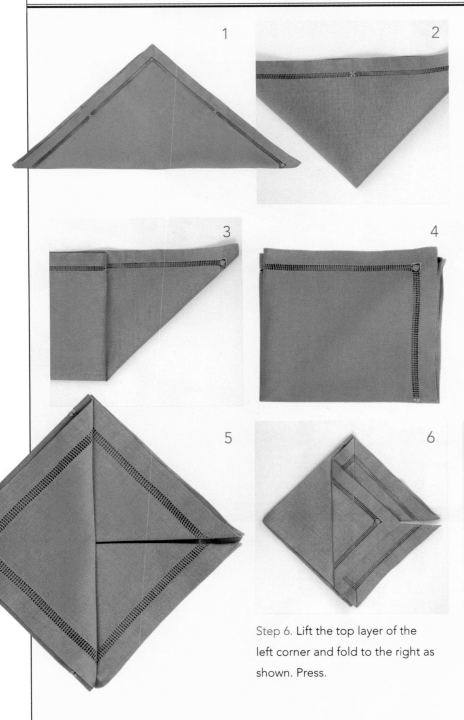

Step 1. With a napkin laid flat, fold diagonally in half, forming a large triangle as shown. Press.

Step 2. Fold the bottom left point over to the bottom right point, creating a smaller triangle. Press. Turn as shown.

Step 3. With right hand, grasp the top layer of fabric by the right point of the triangle. Place left hand under/inside top layer of fabric and pull the right point to the left point, forming a triangle on the right side and a square on the left side.

Step 4. Turn the napkin over and with left hand, grasp the top layer of fabric by the left point. Place right hand under/inside top layer of fabric and pull the left point to the right point, forming a square as shown.

Step 5. Rotate the open corners to the right. Lift up the top layer of fabric from the right and fold to the left point of the diamond. Flip the napkin and repeat with the top layer of fabric.

Step 6. Lift the top layer of the left corner and fold to the right as shown. Press.

Step 7. Tuck the triangle flap of fabric on the left under the napkin.

Step 8. Flip napkin over and overlap both sides in the center. Tuck the top flap into the fold of the bottom flap as shown. Stand napkin upright. If needed, secure with tape or a pin.

the folded holder

Step 1. Complete the Quarter Fold (see page 26). Turn square so the flaps are pointed to the right.

Step 2. Take the top layer from the right and fold over to match the left point.

Steps 3 and 4. Taking the same flap, fold in one inch toward the center, repeating again and again until the edge meets the center fold. Fold the top layer of the right side in a similar manner as shown. Press.

Step 5. Flip the napkin over and fold the top corner down to the center of the napkin diamond.

Steps 6 and 7. Fold the bottom corner up toward the center of the napkin, overlapping the top corner slightly. Press. Flip the napkin over again and tuck a pretty place card in the center slit.

southern lady specialty

Step 1. Complete the Quarter Fold (see page 26).

Step 2. With the open corners pointing toward the bottom, fold the top point down.

Step 3. Turn the napkin over. Fold in the left side at a slight angle, then fold over the opposite side.

Step 4. Turn the napkin over to display a monogram, embellished lace, or a pretty pattern.

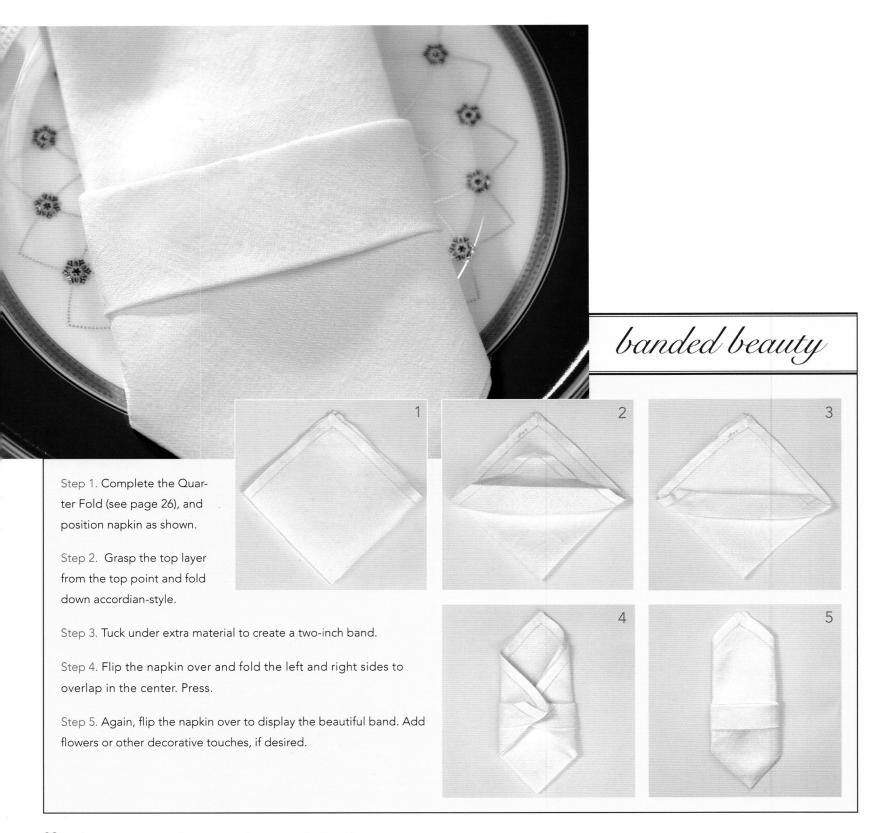

banded beauty

Step 1. Complete the Quarter Fold (see page 26), and position napkin as shown.

Step 2. Grasp the top layer from the top point and fold down accordian-style.

Step 3. Tuck under extra material to create a two-inch band.

Step 4. Flip the napkin over and fold the left and right sides to overlap in the center. Press.

Step 5. Again, flip the napkin over to display the beautiful band. Add flowers or other decorative touches, if desired.

layered lace

Step 1. Complete the Quarter Fold (see page 26), and position napkin as shown.

Step 2. Lift the top layer from the left point and fold back to the right. Similarly fold the next three layers, one at a time, so that pretty edges are displayed as shown.

Step 3. After turning the last decorative layer, press the seam to crease the folds.

the *Entertaining extravaganza*

painting party
Colorful Companions

Whether you're moving into a new residence or simply interested in making your current abode more inviting, a fresh coat of paint and a few dear friends can help turn your house into a home.

Invitations made from color swatches and pint-sized paint cans filled with happy tulips set the tone for this home improvement-themed gathering. Let your creativity be your guide as you search for ways to incorporate brushes, canvas, and hues into your party decorations.

Guests need not worry about what to wear to this relaxed get-together. Casual and comfortable clothing is required attire for this painting adventure that has plenty of fun-filled spill-and-splatter potential.

Teach your companions how to create a textured look on the walls in just a few easy steps, and before you know it, the talk may turn to a repeat of this process at one of your fellow painter's homes. While the paint dries in between treatments, you'll have plenty of time to relax and chat over delicious refreshments.

Palatable treats and a palette of edible paints provide guests with delightful diversions sure to satisfy this hard-working group of starving artists. Expect colorful conversation and vibrant laughter as the afternoon continues, and by the end of the day, you'll find that this time spent together over sweet-n-salty snacks and easy-to-do faux finishes improves not only the appearance of your home but also the friendships you share.

Like a primed canvas just waiting for vibrant splashes and strokes, this sensational home improvement party is filled with promise. Imagine the colorful camaraderie that will emerge when you invite best friends to bond over do-it-yourself painting projects.

Home is your haven, and when it comes to decorating, doing the work yourself adds special meaning. For walls, the slightest changes can take a room from average to elegant, and when your friends join in, the work will be done in no time. So gather your pals, give them a paintbrush, and watch the fun fill the room.

If none among your talented team possesses the faux-finish know-how needed to begin the project, consider bringing in an expert to explain techniques, offer advice, and lead the crew to completion. You'll learn fresh skills, and in the process, you're sure to make a new friend.

Although attention will be focused on actually painting the walls, decorating details help set the perfect party background—a place for both work and play. Bookshelves resembling stepladders showcase snacks and props, while paint cans double as vases for white and yellow tulips. Plates, napkins, and cups in bright greens and oranges remind guests that color is key, a theme that saturates the entire event.

Totable Treats

To thank those helpful hands for pitching in and painting, give guests a miniature memento of the day in the form of a shiny paint can brimming with goodies. Tie a colorful ribbon around the handle and fill the tin with all the supplies needed to make Sugar Cookies with Edible Paint Icing (see page 43). Included in this special assortment are cookie cutters, new brushes, meringue powder, and extra treats, too. You can purchase clean, empty paint cans at your local hardware store, and for an added touch, decorate the outsides with colored paper, ribbons, fringe, buttons, or glitter.

Materials Needed

- Painter's tape
- Water
- 2 to 3 desired colors of interior acrylic paint
- Paint trays
- Various sizes of sea sponges
- Ragging cloths
- White acrylic paint
- Feathers
- Paint rollers and roller covers
- Clear varnishing glaze

Note: *Before you begin, cover the areas you do not wish to paint with painter's tape. Start with a clean, primed wall with a solid base coat. For best results, practice your technique on a sheet of poster board or paper.*

step by step: Faux Finish

Step 1: Wash and rinse sea sponge several times. Wring, and then dip the damp sponge into paint. Squeeze out excess paint to ensure an even coating.

Step 2: Press the sponge lightly and quickly onto the wall, a technique known as sponging on. Be fluid and rotate your angle so the pattern appears random and natural.

Step 3: Before the paint dries, blot with a clean, damp ragging cloth to soften your finish.

When combined with easy-to-learn techniques, everyday tools like sponges, rags, and feathers can create the subtly dramatic illusion of texture.

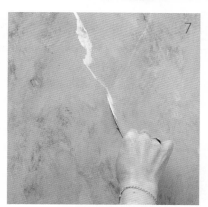

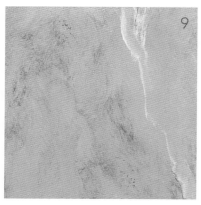

Step 4: Sponging creates wall depth; therefore, the more colors added to a base coat, the greater the effect. Using a new sponge, apply another layer of color to your finish with the same sponging on technique.

Step 5: Blot area with a clean, damp rag. For a different look, experiment with several types of blotting material, such as cheesecloth, netting, linen, or bubble wrap. Allow paints to dry for one to two hours.

Step 6: Natural marble veins flow in the same general direction, although not necessarily parallel. Apply veins in sizes and patterns to suit your project style. Start with two inches of vein color on a clean feather.

Step 7: Begin applying veins in the upper left section of the wall, pulling the feather in a diagonal direction across the surface. Twist and quiver the tip to achieve a natural look. Also, consider veining with darker shades of paint for a shadow effect.

Step 8: If desired, gently roll a thin layer of water-based varnishing glaze over the surface after veins have dried. This technique helps blend your finish and protect your walls.

Step 9: Remove tape from wall within an hour and allow wall to dry completely. The milky coating will appear clear as finisher dries.

Creamy Italian Dip with Fresh Vegetables
Makes 5¹/₂ cups

2 (8-ounce) packages cream cheese, softened
2 (16-ounce) cartons sour cream
2 (0.7-ounce) packages Italian dressing mix
¹/₂ cup chopped green onions
2 cloves garlic, minced
1 teaspoon freshly ground black pepper
6 large carrots, peeled and cut into sticks
4 large zucchini squash, washed and cut into sticks
1 bunch fresh asparagus, washed, ends trimmed and peeled
1 stalk celery, washed, peeled, and cut into sticks
1 head broccoli, washed and cut into florets

■ In a large bowl, combine cream cheese, sour cream, dressing mix, green onions, garlic, and pepper, mixing well. Chill for at least 2 hours. Serve with fresh vegetables.

Creamy Italian Dip with Fresh Vegetables

BLT Rollups

BLT Rollups
Makes 8 servings

¹/₂ cup mayonnaise
¹/₂ cup sour cream
1 tablespoon ranch-style dressing mix
¹/₂ teaspoon freshly ground black pepper
8 sun-dried tomato tortillas
1 pound bacon, cooked and crumbled
1 head green leaf lettuce, washed and shredded
3 medium tomatoes, seeded and chopped

■ In a small bowl, combine mayonnaise, sour cream, dressing mix, and pepper.
■ Evenly spread mayonnaise mixture on 8 tortillas, leaving a ¹/₂-inch border. Layer the lettuce, tomatoes, and bacon on top of mayonnaise mixture.
■ Roll up each tortilla, placing seam on bottom; trim ¹/₄ inch off each end, and slice in half diagonally.

Entertaining Touches

No sense watching the paint dry when there is much relaxing and snacking to be enjoyed. A tin of chilled sodas and platters of filling finger foods offer a satisfying reprieve from a busy bout of work. Take some time to brush up on family happenings and current events while you savor the yummy selections, and soon, you'll be re-energized and ready to finish that stunning second coat.

Crunchy Pasta Party Mix

Rocky Road Fudge

RIGHT: Don't be deceived. These colored mixtures are made for your mouth. Edible Paint Icing is a treat that can complement a variety of confections. With this tasty medium and cookie canvas, partygoers are sure to enjoy the creative process. Pass around small pastry brushes or new, clean craft brushes as well as fresh cups of water—one per color—for rinsing in between shade switching.

Sugar Cookies with Edible Paint Icing

Crunchy Pasta Party Mix

Makes about 9½ cups

1 (16-ounce) package multi-colored pasta (rotini,
    fusilli, farfalle, or other bite-sized pasta)
Vegetable oil (for frying)
½ cup butter, melted
½ cup grated Parmesan cheese
2 tablespoons dried Italian seasoning
1 teaspoon garlic salt

■ Cook pasta according to package directions.
Drain, rinse with cold water, and drain again.
■ Evenly spread cooked pasta onto baking
sheets and let dry for approximately 1 hour.
■ In a large Dutch oven, heat 3 inches of vegetable oil to 365°. Fry pasta, about a dozen at
a time, in hot oil for 1½ to 2 minutes, or until
lightly browned. Remove with slotted spoon
and drain on baking sheets lined with paper
towels. Repeat with remaining pasta, making
sure to maintain oil temperature; cool pasta
completely. Cooked pasta may be stored in an
airtight container for up to 2 days.
■ To serve, combine pasta and butter in a large
bowl; stir to coat. In a separate bowl, combine
Parmesan cheese, Italian seasoning, and garlic
salt. Sprinkle Parmesan seasoning mix over
pasta and toss to coat.

Rocky Road Fudge

Makes 24 servings

3 cups sugar
6 tablespoons margarine
¾ cup evaporated milk
1 (12-ounce) package semisweet chocolate
    morsels
1 (7-ounce) jar marshmallow creme
½ teaspoon vanilla
1 cup chopped pecans
1 cup chopped walnuts
2 cups miniature marshmallows, frozen

■ Line a 9x13-inch pan with aluminum foil;
set aside.
■ In a Dutch oven, heat sugar, margarine, and
milk over medium-high heat. Bring to a boil
and cook, stirring constantly, for 4 minutes.
Remove from heat and stir in chocolate morsels

and marshmallow creme; stir until melted. Stir
in vanilla, pecans, and walnuts.
■ Working quickly, stir in frozen marshmallows
just until coated. Immediately spread in an even
layer in prepared pan. Cool completely and cut
into 24 squares.

Sugar Cookies with Edible Paint Icing

Makes about 2½ dozen

1½ cups sugar
1 cup butter, softened
2 large eggs
1 teaspoon vanilla extract
4½ cups all-purpose flour
1 teaspoon baking powder
1 teaspoon baking soda
½ teaspoon salt
1 cup sour cream
1 recipe Edible Paint Icing (recipe follows)

■ In a large mixing bowl, combine sugar and butter. Beat at medium speed with an electric mixer
until fluffy. Add eggs and vanilla, beating well.
■ In a medium bowl, combine flour, baking
powder, baking soda, and salt. Add to sugar mixture alternately with sour cream, beginning and
ending with flour mixture. Beat at low speed,
blending well after each addition.
■ Divide dough into thirds; wrap each portion
in plastic wrap and refrigerate 2 hours.
■ Preheat oven to 400°. Line a baking sheet
with parchment paper; set aside.
■ On lightly floured surface, roll each portion
of chilled dough to ¼-inch thickness. Cut out
shapes with cookie cutters. Place 1 inch apart
on prepared baking sheet. Bake for 7 to 9
minutes, or until edges are lightly browned.
Transfer to wire racks to cool. Decorate with
Edible Paint Icing.

Edible Paint Icing:

Makes about 2 cups

½ cup cold water
¼ cup meringue powder
3 cups confectioners' sugar
Food coloring paste

Smart Cookies

Step out of the mold. Cookie
cutters now come in numerous
shapes so you can make a house,
a mailbox, a tree, and a multitude
of other cutouts to suit most any
occasion. For your painting party,
invite friends to bring their own
shapes from home so you can mix,
match, and munch your way to a
perfectly happy day.

■ In a large mixing bowl, beat water and meringue powder at medium speed with an electric
mixer until stiff peaks form. Add confectioners'
sugar and continue beating on low speed until
blended.
■ To store icing, spoon into a container with a
tight-fitting lid. Place heavy-duty plastic wrap
over container, pressing down plastic wrap until
it touches the entire surface of the icing. Seal
container with lid. Beat icing at medium speed
with electric mixer before use.
■ If coloring icing, divide into smaller bowls
and add food coloring paste until desired color
is achieved. Small amounts of cold water may
be added to adjust icing to desired consistency
for painting cookies. Icing will dry hard.

porch party

The Spice of Life

The epitome of outdoor entertaining, a convivial porch party, complete with tantalizing Cajun-inspired cuisine, offers an abundance of ways to enjoy an evening spent in the splendor of autumn allurement.

Changing leaves in shades of red, yellow, and orange rustle in the trees like jewel-toned confetti. Further hints of festivity are found in the pumpkins, gourds, squash, mums, and hay that line the walkway leading to the back porch. Here guests discover an autumnal wonderland of wooden rocking chairs, soft patchwork quilts, and dishes so delicious that they entice each and every person in attendance.

Zesty appetizers please the palate, and incredible cocktails—including a dangerously delightful version of a Southern staple aptly named Spiked Sweet Tea—keep everyone guessing about what could possibly top such

sweet and savory selections. But spicy Chicken and Sausage Gumbo does the trick, as does its successor, ooey-gooey Sweet Potato Gingerbread with Maple Pecan Butter Sauce.

Rich tones of autumn entice the well-fed partygoers to retire from the table into wicker swings and cushioned chairs where they can relax and enjoy the view. Tall tales and witty anecdotes add to the colorful atmosphere while children take to the backyard to rouse a few piles of leaves. Laughter persists, and all agree, the porch may well be the best place to admire the arrival of fall.

Fabulous Fall

Shiny apples of red and green. Paper-like leaves of golden yellow. Round persimmons and tall pumpkins of the boldest orange. Yes, Mother Nature's color palette offers bountiful inspiration for this fabulous fall shindig. Large glass hurricane containers showcase treasured harvest hues—as well as a few tasty treats—while Hurricane Punch prompts a toast to the kick off of this season favored for its college football and fabulous foliage. Comfortable rocking chairs provide a place to sit and rest, where folks can settle into the steady rhythm of familiar back-and-forth creaking, reveling in idyllic scenery and autumnal bliss .

Roasted Garlic Bread

Roasted Garlic Bread

Makes 10 to 12 servings

3 heads garlic, unpeeled
2 tablespoons olive oil
$1/2$ cup butter, softened
2 tablespoons chopped fresh parsley
1 teaspoon fresh lemon juice
1 teaspoon crushed red pepper flakes (optional)
1 large loaf French bread, sliced in half lengthwise

■ Preheat oven to 425°. Place garlic on aluminum foil. Drizzle garlic with olive oil. Fold edges of foil together to seal. Bake 30 minutes; cool. Reduce heat to 375°.
■ Cut top off garlic heads and squeeze cooked garlic into a small bowl. Add butter, parsley, lemon juice, and red pepper flakes; stirring to mix well. Spread both halves of bread with butter mixture.
■ Bake 15 to 20 minutes, or until bread is lightly browned. To serve, slice bread into $1^{1}/_{2}$-inch-wide slices; serve warm.

Louisiana Crab Dip

Makes about 6 cups

2 (8-ounce) packages cream cheese, softened
1 cup sour cream
3 tablespoons fresh lemon juice
$1^{1}/_{2}$ tablespoons Creole seasoning
2 teaspoons dried minced onion
$1/4$ cup finely chopped green onion
2 tablespoons chopped fresh parsley
1 tablespoon hot sauce (optional)
$1/4$ teaspoon salt
3 (8-ounce) cartons fresh lump crabmeat, picked for shells

Louisiana Crab Dip

Shrimp Crostini with Creole Cream Sauce

■ In a medium bowl, combine cream cheese, sour cream, lemon juice, Creole seasoning, and dried onion. Beat at medium speed with an electric mixer until well blended. Add green onion, parsley, hot sauce, and salt, stirring to mix well. Stir in crabmeat just until combined. Cover and chill. Serve with crackers.

Entertaining Touches

Earthy pottery and printed napkins help create the casual and carefree feel of this party that packs plenty of panache. Begin with tantalizing appetizers in the late afternoon so you'll have the entire evening to enjoy the virtues of and view from the porch.

Shrimp Crostini with Creole Cream Sauce

Makes 12 servings

1 French baguette
½ cup plus 2 tablespoons butter, divided
1 pound medium fresh shrimp, peeled and de-
    veined
2 tablespoons plus 2 teaspoons Creole seasoning,
    divided
1 red bell pepper, chopped
1 tablespoon minced garlic
¼ cup lemon juice
2 teaspoons Worcestershire sauce
1⅓ cups heavy whipping cream
2 teaspoons hot sauce (optional)
¼ cup chopped green onion
2 tablespoons chopped fresh parsley
Garnish: chopped fresh parsley, chopped green
onion

■ Preheat oven to 350°.
■ Cut baguette into 24 (½-inch) slices. Spread both sides of each baguette slice with butter. Place on a baking sheet and bake 5 to 10 minutes, or until golden around the edges; set aside.
■ Combine shrimp and 2 tablespoons Creole seasoning in a small bowl; set aside. In a large skillet, melt 2 tablespoons butter over medium heat. Add red pepper and garlic; cook 2 to 3 minutes until pepper becomes soft.
■ Add shrimp and cook 2 minutes on each side. Add lemon juice, 2 teaspoons Creole seasoning, Worcestershire sauce, cream, and hot sauce. Simmer for 5 minutes. Remove from heat; stir in green onion and parsley.
■ To serve, spoon 3 to 4 shrimp onto each crostini; top shrimp with about 2 tablespoons sauce. Garnish with parsley and green onions, if desired.

RIGHT: A centerpiece made with finds from a backyard scavenger hunt proves to be quite an interesting and inexpensive addition to the setting. By incorporating a few purchased squash and gourds, you'll achieve an arrangement that pays appropriate homage to enchanting autumn.

Tasso Ham Turnovers with Roasted Red Pepper Remoulade

Peanut Butter Pecan Pralines

ABOVE: When you mix together peanut butter and pecans, the results are sure to please, especially when they're in the form of pralines. You may want to consider adding a few other kid-friendly dishes to the menu since this party is designed with spice in mind. For ideas, see the recipes featured in the Fairytale Birthday party on page 86.

Chicken and Sausage Gumbo

Tasso Ham Turnovers with Roasted Red Pepper Remoulade
Makes 2 dozen

1/4 cup olive oil
1/2 cup finely chopped onion
1/4 cup finely chopped green bell pepper
1/4 cup finely chopped celery
2 cloves garlic, minced
1 cup finely chopped tasso ham
1 large egg
1 tablespoon water
2 (17.3-ounce) boxes frozen puff pastry, thawed
1/2 cup grated Monterey Jack cheese
1 recipe Roasted Red Pepper Remoulade (recipe follows)

- In a large sauté pan, heat oil over medium-high heat. Add onion, green pepper, and celery; cook 4 to 5 minutes, or until tender. Add garlic and cook 1 minute. Add ham and cook 2 minutes. Remove from heat; cool 10 minutes.
- Preheat oven to 400°. Line 2 baking sheets with parchment paper; set aside.
- In a small bowl, whisk together egg and water; set aside.
- On a lightly floured surface, roll out each pastry sheet to a 12x14-inch rectangle. Using a 3-inch round cutter, cut 12 circles from each sheet of puff pastry. Spoon 1 teaspoon tasso mixture in the center of half of pastry circles; top tasso mixture with about 1 teaspoon cheese.
- With a pastry brush, brush outside edge of prepared pastry circles. Top with remaining pastry circles to enclose filling, pressing edges to seal. Using a fork, crimp edges. With a small knife, make a small slit in top of each turnover to allow steam to escape during baking.
- Place on prepared baking sheets and bake 12 to 14 minutes, or until golden brown. Cool for 5 minutes before serving. Serve with Roasted Red Pepper Remoulade.

Roasted Red Pepper Remoulade:
Makes about 2 cups

1 cup mayonnaise
1 (7.25-ounce) jar roasted red peppers, drained
2 tablespoons Creole mustard
2 tablespoons ketchup
2 tablespoons sweet pickle relish
1 tablespoon capers, rinsed and drained
1 tablespoon chopped fresh parsley
1 green onion, chopped

- In work bowl of a food processor, combine mayonnaise, roasted red peppers, mustard, and ketchup; process until smooth. Add remaining ingredients, and pulse until onion is minced, but not pureed. Cover and chill.

Chicken and Sausage Gumbo
Makes 10 to 12 servings

12 cups water
4 skinless bone-in chicken breasts
2 medium yellow onions, quartered
3 ribs celery, cut into large pieces
3 bay leaves
1 tablespoon salt
1 tablespoon Creole seasoning
1 1/2 cups all-purpose flour
1 1/2 cups vegetable oil
2 cups diced yellow onion
1/2 cup chopped green bell pepper
1/2 cup chopped red bell pepper
1 cup chopped celery
2 pounds Andouille (Cajun) sausage, cut into 1/2-inch slices
1/4 cup chopped green onions
1/4 cup chopped fresh parsley
Hot cooked rice
Garnish: hot sauce, cayenne pepper

- In a Dutch oven, combine first seven ingredients over high heat and bring to a boil. Reduce heat to medium and cook until chicken is tender (about 45 minutes). Remove chicken and cool 10 minutes. Pull chicken from bones, and chop into bite-size pieces; cover and refrigerate until ready to use. Strain broth, discarding solids, and set aside.
- In a Dutch oven, combine flour and oil over medium-high heat. Whisking constantly, cook for 15 to 20 minutes, until flour mixture turns dark brown. Add onion, green pepper, red pepper, celery, and sausage, stirring to mix well. Add reserved chicken broth, and stir until well combined. Bring to a boil; reduce heat to medium-low and cook uncovered for 1 1/2 hours, stirring occasionally.

- Add chicken and cook for 15 minutes. Remove from heat and let stand for 5 minutes. Skim surface to remove any fat. Stir in green onions and parsley and serve with hot cooked rice. Garnish with hot sauce and cayenne pepper, if desired.

Peanut Butter Pecan Pralines
Makes about 1 1/2 dozen

1 cup sugar
1 cup firmly packed light brown sugar
1 cup evaporated milk
1/4 cup salted butter, softened
1/3 cup creamy peanut butter
1 1/2 cups chopped pecans
1 teaspoon vanilla

- In a large, heavy-bottomed saucepan or Dutch oven, combine sugars and milk over medium-high heat. Stir constantly until mixture reaches 228° on a candy thermometer. Add butter, peanut butter, and pecans and continue to stir until mixture reaches 240° on the candy thermometer.
- Remove from heat, and stir in vanilla. Beat vigorously with a wooden spoon until mixture begins to thicken and lose its glossy appearance. Working quickly, drop by rounded tablespoonfuls onto aluminum foil.
- Cool completely and store in an airtight container.

Spiked Sweet Tea

ABOVE: Tiny hands can't get enough of sweet treats, but Spiked Sweet Tea is reserved for the adults in attendance. One sip is all it takes to become completely enthralled with this innovative twist on a Southern staple.

RIGHT: Though a warm drizzle of Maple Pecan Butter Sauce will certainly top off your Sweet Potato Gingerbread in a most delicious way, an extra spoonful—or two— only adds to its appeal.

Sweet Potato Gingerbread with Maple Pecan Butter Sauce

Spiked Sweet Tea
Makes about 1 gallon

3 quarts cold water, divided
3 family-size tea bags
$^1/_2$ cup fresh mint leaves
$1^1/_2$ cups sugar
1 (12-ounce can) frozen pink lemonade
  concentrate, thawed
1 cup citrus-flavored vodka
Garnish: fresh lemon slices, fresh mint sprigs

■ In a medium saucepan, bring 1 quart water to a boil. Remove from heat and add tea bags and mint; cover and steep 5 minutes. Strain tea into large container, and stir in sugar until dissolved. Add lemonade, vodka, and remaining water; stir to mix. Cover and chill. Serve over ice. Garnish with lemon slices and mint sprigs, if desired.

Sweet Potato Gingerbread with Maple Pecan Butter Sauce
Makes 12 servings

$2^1/_2$ cups all-purpose flour
$1^1/_2$ teaspoons baking soda
$1^1/_2$ teaspoons ground ginger
1 teaspoon baking powder
1 teaspoon salt
$^1/_2$ teaspoon ground cinnamon
$1^1/_4$ cups firmly packed light brown sugar
$^1/_2$ cup butter, softened
1 cup cooked mashed sweet potato
$^1/_2$ cup evaporated milk
$^1/_4$ cup dark molasses
2 large eggs
1 teaspoon vanilla extract
1 recipe Maple Pecan Butter Sauce (recipe
  follows)

■ Preheat oven to 350°. Grease and flour a 13x9x2-inch pan; set aside.
■ In a medium bowl, sift together flour, baking soda, ginger, baking powder, salt, and cinnamon; set aside.
■ In a large mixing bowl, combine sugar and butter; beat with an electric mixer at medium speed until creamy. Add sweet potato, milk,

molasses, eggs, and vanilla, beating to mix well. Gradually add flour mixture to sweet potato mixture, beating until combined.
■ Spoon batter into prepared pan. Bake for 30 to 40 minutes, or until a wooden pick inserted in center comes out clean. Cool in pan for 10 minutes. Remove from pan and cut into 12 squares. Serve warm with Maple Pecan Butter Sauce.

Maple Pecan Butter Sauce:
Makes about 2 cups

1 cup maple syrup
$^1/_2$ cup butter, cut into pieces
$^1/_4$ cup sugar
1 large egg, lightly beaten
1 tablespoon vanilla extract
1 cup pecan pieces

■ In a medium saucepan, combine maple syrup, butter, sugar, and egg over medium heat. Simmer mixture 6 minutes, whisking constantly. Remove from heat and stir in vanilla. Just before serving, stir in pecans. Serve warm.

Hurricane Punch
Makes 6 to 8 servings

1 cup sugar
1 cup water
4 cups pineapple juice
4 cups orange juice
2 cups light rum
1 cup grenadine
$^1/_2$ cup fresh lemon juice
$^1/_2$ cup fresh lime juice
$^1/_4$ cup Triple Sec
1 teaspoon almond extract
1 liter ginger ale or lemon-lime-flavored
  carbonated beverage, chilled

■ In a small saucepan, combine sugar and water over medium heat. Bring to a boil, stirring until sugar dissolves. Cool completely.
■ In a large pitcher, combine sugar syrup and next 8 ingredients; stir to mix well. When ready to serve, add ginger ale or lemon-lime beverage; stir gently. Serve over ice.

Hurricane Punch

Refreshing Twist

Light and refreshing, Hurricane Punch can be served throughout the year and is a nice alternative to traditional punch recipes. You can easily prepare a nonalcoholic version of this drink by simply making a few changes and substitutions. First, add an extra cup of both sugar and water to your ingredient list, for a total of two cups each. Next, eliminate the rum and Triple Sec. Follow the remainder of the instructions according to the original recipe, and within minutes, you'll have a delicious beverage that will please the entire crowd.

evening elegance
The Black & White Party

Dramatic in every sense of the word, the unparalleled contrast of black and white paired with the utmost in style and sophistication sets the stage for an evening affair to last the ages.

Divine and sublime describe the almost electric ambiance created by the timeless combination of deepest black and purest white. Place this daring duo front and center as the theme for a brilliant black-tie assemblage of your closest circle of friends.

It's your time to shine as the ultimate hostess by bringing out the best of the best—your finest china, crystal, and silver. Artful flower arrangements featuring varieties of white and cream lilies up the elegance of the table as onyx accents heighten the aesthetic appeal. Adding to this magnificent cast, lavish cocktails and an

incredible menu tempt even the most refined taste buds, surely sending your guests into rounds of applause.

Talented fingers tickle the ivory keys of a baby grand piano, and all those in attendance, pressed and dressed to perfection, bask in the spotlight of this special night. On this occasion, each and every guest feels like a star, showered with adoration and appreciation in the form of absolutely royal treatment. Raised glasses of champagne toast the moment into a memory that will forever celebrate the exquisite entertainment and fine dining of a formal fête.

Showstoppers

Over-the-top arrangements of stark white and creamy ivory with hints of the lightest greens elevate the dining table to award-worthy status. Striped candles make a special appearance, giving an unexpected edge to this impressive evening presentation.

Places Please

Glitz and glamour stem from twelve sets of crystal glasses, and as part of the supporting cast, silver flatware adds elements of sparkle and shine. Though not appearing in their traditional role, sterling knife rests perform well as place-card holders in this dinnertime spectacular.

Regal Reprise

Elegant china adorned with flowing black-ribbon details provides the perfect place to stage the most anticipated part of the night—the five-course meal. When dinner and drinks are finished, tuxedo take-home gifts entice guests to enjoy an encore of sorts even after the curtains close on this exciting event.

The theme of black and white becomes the script for this glamorous gala for twelve, but improvisation and imagination are the keys to achieving critical acclaim.

From the checkerboard floor to the 88 piano keys, black and white echo their elegance in a number of ways. Pristine tablecloths and linens garner noteworthy nods, while signature cocktails receive continual praise.

Sleek and sophisticated, the dress for this formal affair also helps to create the stylish ambiance. Guests choose their favorite fashions within the slated color scheme, their very presence in a given room immediately and chicly adding to the décor. When all in attendance take their seats around the table, the party's theme reveals itself even more as a star-studded meal is served to the utmost satisfaction.

Menu

Black and White Russian

Champagne

Dilled Potato Pancakes with Smoked Salmon

Lobster and Hearts of Palm Salad with Blood Orange Vinaigrette

Lemon Buttermilk Sorbet

Beef Tenderloin with Madeira Reduction

White Truffle Risotto

Sautéed Swiss Chard

Chocolate Sushi

Black and White Russian

Entertaining Touches

When hosting such a formal affair, you may want to consider hiring a chef to prepare the delectable recipes and a staff to serve them. This will allow you to enjoy the night just as much as your guests as you all partake of dishes that are nothing short of divine.

Dilled Potato Pancakes with Smoked Salmon

Lobster and Hearts of Palm Salad with Blood Orange Vinaigrette

Black and White Russian
Makes 1 serving

2 ounces half-and-half
1 ounce Godiva White Chocolate Liqueur®
1 ounce Godiva Cappuccino Liqueur®
1/4 ounce vodka

Combine all ingredients. Serve over ice.

Dilled Potato Pancakes with Smoked Salmon
Makes 12 servings

2 large eggs, beaten
1/2 cup grated onion, drained completely
1/4 cup flour
2 tablespoons chopped fresh dill
1 1/2 teaspoons salt
1/4 teaspoon ground black pepper

5 medium potatoes
1/2 cup vegetable oil, divided
1 (4-ounce) package smoked salmon
Garnish: sour cream or crème fraîche, black caviar, fresh dill sprigs

■ In a large bowl, combine eggs, onion, flour, dill, salt, and pepper; stir to mix well. Peel and grate potatoes; pat dry with paper towels and immediately combine with egg mixture.
■ In a 10-inch non-stick skillet, heat 1/4 cup oil over medium heat. Drop mixture by heaping tablespoonfuls into skillet. Cook for 4 to 5 minutes on each side, until golden brown; drain on paper towels. Add additional oil as needed.
■ Top each pancake with a thin slice of salmon. Garnish with sour cream or crème fraiche, caviar, and fresh dill sprigs, if desired.

Note: To prepare these a day in advance, cook as directed and refrigerate overnight. Preheat oven to 400°. Place pancakes on a wire rack on a baking sheet. Bake for 10 to 15 minutes or until crispy.

Lobster and Hearts of Palm Salad with Blood Orange Vinaigrette

Makes 12 servings

2 (5-ounce) bags spring salad mix or mesclun
  salad mix
4 (8 to10-ounce) cooked lobster tails, sliced
6 blood oranges, sectioned
2 (14-ounce) cans hearts of palm, drained and
  sliced
1 recipe Blood Orange Vinaigrette (recipe follows)
Garnish: poppy seeds

■ Evenly divide salad greens, lobster, oranges, and hearts of palm on each of 12 salad plates. Drizzle with Blood Orange Vinaigrette and garnish with poppy seeds, if desired.

Blood Orange Vinaigrette:

Makes 2 cups

1 cup fresh blood orange juice
1 shallot, minced
¼ cup honey
2 tablespoons white-wine vinegar
1 teaspoon Dijon mustard
½ teaspoon salt
¼ teaspoon ground black pepper
½ cup vegetable oil

■ In container of an electric blender, combine all ingredients except oil; process until blended. With blender running, add oil in a slow, steady stream; process until blended.

RIGHT: The White Truffle Risotto served alongside Beef Tenderloin and Sautéed Swiss Chard takes its unique taste from white truffle oil, which is available at gourmet markets. The distinct flavor adds richness to a variety of foods, including salad dressings and mashed potatoes. Complementing this richness, champagne also enhances the other delicious dishes featured in this party.

Beef Tenderloin with Madeira Reduction
White Truffle Risotto
Sautéed Swiss Chard

Lemon Buttermilk Sorbet

Beef Tenderloin with Madeira Reduction

Chocolate Sushi

ABOVE: To cleanse the palate, a tiny scoop of Lemon Buttermilk Sorbet is enjoyed just before the beef entrée, but this recipe can also be served in larger portions as a dessert for your next summertime soiree.

RIGHT: A masterpiece of culinary creativity, Chocolate Sushi takes its name from its shape. Chocolate and cream combine in the sweetest way, and varied toppings add even more posh and trendy finale options.

Lemon Buttermilk Sorbet
Makes about 5 cups

2 cups sugar
2 cups water
1½ cups fresh lemon juice
1 cup buttermilk
2 tablespoons grated lemon zest
Garnish: lemon zest

- In a medium saucepan, combine sugar and water over medium heat. Cook 10 minutes, stirring frequently, until sugar is completely dissolved; cool completely.
- In a large bowl, combine sugar syrup and remaining ingredients.
- Place mixture in ice cream freezer and freeze according to manufacturer's instructions, until firm; store in freezer.
- To serve, spoon sorbet into bowl or glass and garnish with lemon zest, if desired.

Beef Tenderloin with Madeira Reduction
Makes 12 servings

3 tablespoons olive oil
1 tablespoon minced garlic
½ teaspoon salt
¼ teaspoon ground black pepper
1 (5½ to 6-pound) beef tenderloin, trimmed
1 recipe Madeira Reduction (recipe follows)

- Preheat oven to 450°. In a small bowl, combine olive oil, garlic, salt, and pepper. Rub on outside of tenderloin. Place on rack in roasting pan and roast for 20 minutes.
- Reduce heat to 350°. Cook for 20 to 25 minutes, or until a meat thermometer inserted into center reaches 145° (medium), or desired degree of doneness. Cool 10 minutes and cut into thin slices.

Madeira Reduction:
Makes about 2½ cups

4 tablespoons butter, divided
3 shallots, minced
4 cups Madeira wine
2 cups chicken broth
¼ teaspoon salt
¼ teaspoon ground black pepper

- In a Dutch oven, melt 2 tablespoons butter over medium-high heat. Add shallot, and sauté 2 to 3 minutes. Add Madeira and bring to a simmer; cook for 5 minutes. Add chicken broth, salt, and pepper; continue to simmer until sauce reduces by half, about 20 to 25 minutes. Whisk in remaining butter.

White Truffle Risotto
Makes 12 servings

4 tablespoons butter, divided
2 tablespoons olive oil
½ cup finely chopped onion
3½ cups Arborio rice
3 quarts hot chicken broth
1 cup freshly grated Parmesan cheese
¼ teaspoon ground white pepper
Garnish: white truffle oil

- In a Dutch oven, heat 2 tablespoons butter and olive oil over medium heat. Add onion; cook 2 to 3 minutes, stirring constantly. Add rice; cook 2 to 3 minutes, or until very lightly browned, stirring constantly. Add hot chicken broth, ¼ cup at a time, allowing liquid to be absorbed after each addition, stirring constantly.
- Repeat procedure until rice becomes creamy in texture, about 30 to 35 minutes.
- Remove from heat and stir in cheese and remaining butter. Drizzle with white truffle oil, if desired.

Sautéed Swiss Chard
Makes 10 to 12 servings

6 pounds Swiss chard (about 6 bunches)
4 tablespoons olive oil, divided
4 tablespoons butter, divided
2 teaspoons minced garlic, divided
4 tablespoons balsamic vinegar, divided
½ teaspoon salt, divided
½ teaspoon ground black pepper, divided

- Remove stalks and roughly chop Swiss chard leaves.
- In a large Dutch oven, heat 2 tablespoons olive oil over medium-high heat. Add 1 teaspoon garlic and half of Swiss chard leaves, tossing to coat with oil, until wilted. Stir in 2 tablespoons vinegar, ¼ teaspoon salt, and ¼ teaspoon pepper. Set aside. Repeat procedure with remaining ingredients.

Chocolate Sushi
Makes 1½ dozen

8 large eggs, separated
1½ cups sugar, divided
2 tablespoons butter
½ cup bittersweet chocolate morsels
½ teaspoon vanilla extract
1 recipe Chantilly Cream (recipe follows)
½ cup cocoa powder
Garnish: fresh raspberries

- Preheat oven to 350°. Generously grease a 14x10-inch jelly-roll pan; set aside.
- In a medium bowl, combine egg yolks and 1 cup sugar; beat at medium speed with an electric mixer until light and fluffy, 2 to 3 minutes.
- In a small saucepan, melt butter over low heat; stir in chocolate until melted and smooth. Add vanilla, stirring well to combine; cool slightly.
- In a medium bowl, beat egg whites at medium speed with an electric mixer until soft peaks form. Gradually add remaining sugar and beat until stiff peaks form.
- Combine chocolate mixture with egg mixture; mix until well combined. Gently fold in egg whites in thirds until well combined.
- Spoon batter into prepared pan. Bake 15 minutes; cool completely. Freeze cake 2 or more hours.
- With a serrated knife, cut cake into 1½ x 2-inch pieces. Spread center with Chantilly Cream, leaving a ½-inch border; gently roll into a cylinder to enclose filling.
- Freeze 2 or more hours; gently roll each cylinder in cocoa powder. Garnish with fresh raspberries. Refrigerate until ready to serve.

Chantilly Cream:
Makes about 1 cup

⅔ cup heavy whipping cream
1 teaspoon vanilla extract
¼ cup sugar

- In a medium mixing bowl, combine cream and vanilla. Beat at medium speed with an electric mixer 1 minute. Gradually add sugar and beat until soft peaks form. Refrigerate until ready to use.

wine & dine

Taste of Tuscany

The melding of exquisite aromas and superb flavors set against the backdrop of a sophisticated evening of spirited discussion and refined repartee—an Italian-inspired wine tasting embodies the essence of tasteful entertaining.

A wooden table laden with fine cheeses, ripe fruits, and freshly baked breads entices company to pull up a chair and partake of this bountiful feast for the eyes as well as the stomach. Rustic brick walls highlighted by the masterful design of sleek archways showcase even more choice offerings—a vast selection of wines.

This occasion features carefully chosen bottles from the Tuscan countryside paired with mouthwatering cheese tortas. One at a time, bottles are uncorked, releasing the juice of grapes, a concoction that has long been referred to as the nectar of the gods. Sipping slowly, members of the group, feeling somewhat like royalty themselves, revel in emerging aromas and mingling flavors. Crackers, breads, and biscotti are passed around in abundance as each person shares in the pleasure of these palatable delights.

Literary works and historical happenings become the topics of conversation, as do the various beverages that have been poured and swirled to perfection. Reds, whites, and sensuously sweet dessert wines saturate the entire experience with an intoxicatingly splendid series of candid exchanges and varied tastes so refined.

What pleasure and perfection, what complexity and connectedness—all bursting forth from that sensuous fruit, the grape.

Uncork your creativity for this Italian-inspired soiree. From the fruits and flowers to the flavors and favors, there are many ways in which you can enhance the wine-tasting experience.

A small slit carefully cut into the side of one cork can transform a bottle stopper into a fun way to display dish descriptors and quotable quips, or use a collection of corks for serving by securing the stoppers inside of a basic four-sided tray. Even a presentation of corked wines to be sampled throughout the evening heightens the romantically rustic ambiance of this classic and cultured social assembly.

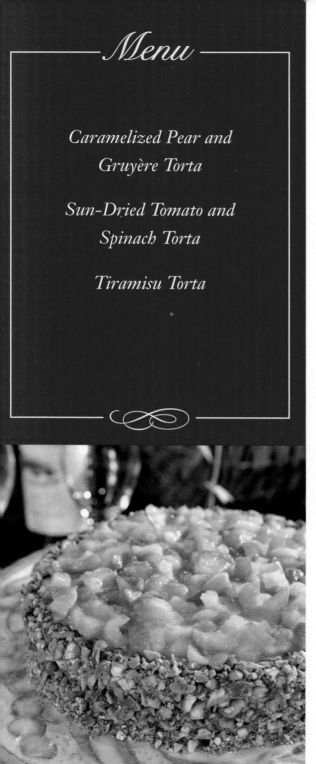

Menu

*Caramelized Pear and
Gruyère Torta*

*Sun-Dried Tomato and
Spinach Torta*

Tiramisu Torta

Caramelized Pear and Gruyère Torta

Though serving wine involves distinctive details—the right food pairings, the optimum temperatures, and even the best-suited glasses for the premium taste—there is no need to feel intimidated. Many books are available on the subject, and your local wine shop can prove a valuable resource as well. And because today's market features a wide selection of wines that are both excellent and affordable, you needn't worry about purchasing bottles that will break the budget. Remember, the main purpose of this party is to eat, drink, and be merry.

Caramelized Pear and Gruyère Torta
Makes 1 (8-inch) torta

2 tablespoons butter
1/2 cup sugar
4 large green D'Anjou pears, chopped
4 (8-ounce) packages Neufchâtel cheese, softened
2 cups grated Gruyère cheese
1 cup chopped pistachio nuts

■ In a large sauté pan, melt butter over medium-high heat. Stir in sugar and pears until well combined. Cook for 12 to 15 minutes until liquid thickens, and pears begin to caramelize. Remove from heat; set aside and cool completely.
■ In a medium mixing bowl, combine Neufchatel cheese and Gruyère cheese. Beat with an electric mixer at medium speed until well combined.
■ Line a round 8-inch cake pan with plastic wrap. Spread half of cheese mixture in bottom of pan. Spread half of pear mixture in pan; top with remaining cheese mixture; refrigerate for 1 hour.
■ Invert onto serving dish and remove from pan. Carefully remove plastic wrap. Cover sides of torta with pistachio nuts; top with remaining pears. Cover and refrigerate until ready to serve. Serve with crackers.

Sun-Dried Tomato and Spinach Torta
Makes 1 (8-inch) torta

4 (8-ounce) packages cream cheese, softened
1 1/2 cups grated Parmesan cheese
3/4 cup crumbled feta cheese
1 teaspoon garlic powder
1 cup frozen spinach, thawed and drained completely
1 cup chopped sun-dried tomatoes
1 cup toasted pine nuts
1 (3-ounce) jar prepared pesto

■ In a large mixing bowl, combine cream cheese, Parmesan cheese, feta cheese, and garlic powder. Beat with an electric mixer at medium speed until well combined. Divide cream cheese mixture into thirds. Combine one-third cheese mixture and spinach; set aside.
■ Line a round 8-inch cake pan with plastic wrap. Spread one-third cream cheese mixture in bottom of pan. Layer half of tomatoes on cheese. Spread spinach mixture on top of tomatoes. Layer remaining tomatoes on top of spinach mixture. Top with remaining cheese mixture; refrigerate for 1 hour.
■ Invert onto serving dish and remove from pan. Carefully remove plastic wrap. Cover sides of torta with pine nuts. Spread pesto on top of torta. Cover and refrigerate until ready to serve. Serve with crackers.

Perfectly Pairable

perfectly pairable

This trio of tortas was created with entertaining ease in mind. Hearty red wines pair best with Sun-Dried Tomato and Spinach Torta, complementing the cheese's strong flavors, while the creamy and sweet Caramelized Pear and Gruyère Torta calls for crisp white wine. End the evening with dessert wines and the Tiramisu Torta. Searching for suggestions? Here are a few affordable options that will bring a Tuscan taste to the table:

WHITE:
2004 Quirico Vernaccia di San Gimignano

Producer of the highest classification of white wine in Tuscany, Quirico's Vernaccia is characterized by its crisp, dry, and refreshing acidity.

RED:
2001 Le Cinciole Chianti Classico

Traditionally a very smooth Chianti, Le Cinciole's version still has the characteristic earthy tannin and subtle acidity that makes the wine food-friendly.

DESSERT:
2000 Villa la Selva "Vigna del Papa" Vin Santo

Before they are pressed, harvested grapes for Vin Santo are dried on straw mats for up to four months. The super-ripe, sweet juice gathered from the grapes creates a dessert wine known for its intensely concentrated lush texture. Dipping biscotti in this wine is a delicious Italian tradition that remains popular today.

Sun-Dried Tomato and Spinach Torta

Simply Charming

Don't play a guessing game of whose is whose. Unique to each glass, wine charms are whimsical ways to accessorize and identify your stemware. Make your own in a few simple steps. First, string stand-alone stones or pretty patterns of beads onto earring hoops. Available at craft stores, these wires come pre-made with an eyelet on the end to clasp around your glass. When your trinket is complete, use chain nose pliers to bend the tip of the wire, locking in the beads and creating a hook for the hoop. No longer dependent on telltale traces of lipstick, you'll be able to spot your stem from across the room—and guests will love the charming reminder of one classy night.

Pretty & Practical

Hard to imagine, yes, but sometimes even the most wonderful of wines must be savored another day. Wine stoppers are essential accessories to sealing leftover libations and keeping selections fresh for days to come. Both pretty and practical, stoppers also serve as fun favors. Accompanied by a choice bottle of wine or individually wrapped in raffia and ribbon, extra embellishments come in a variety of dazzling designs. From blown glass and sparkling gems to shaped clay and whittled wood, these favor finds are true showstoppers. Other sure-to-be-treasured tokens are take-home notecards listing names and descriptions of sampled wines. After noting their favorites, guests can tuck these lists into purses for safekeeping until the next market visit.

Tiramisu Torta

Makes 1 (6-inch) torta

2 tablespoons butter
1 cup chopped hazelnuts
¹/₄ cup sugar
¹/₄ cup water
1 (8-ounce) package cream cheese, softened
¹/₄ cup confectioners' sugar
2 (8-ounce) containers tiramisu-flavored mascarpone cheese, softened
³/₄ cup coarsely grated chocolate

■ In a medium sauté pan, melt butter over medium-high heat. Stir in hazelnuts, sugar, and water. Cook for approximately 7 minutes, until the nuts are toasted and syrup coats nuts evenly. Spread nuts on parchment paper. Using a fork, separate nuts and cool completely. Coating will harden.

■ In a medium bowl, beat cream cheese and confectioners' sugar with an electric mixer at medium speed, until smooth; set aside.

■ Line a round 6-inch cake pan with plastic wrap. Spread half of mascarpone cheese on bottom of pan. Sprinkle with one-third grated chocolate. Spread cream cheese mixture on top of chocolate layer. Sprinkle with one-third grated chocolate. Spread remaining mascarpone cheese in pan; refrigerate for 1 hour.

■ Invert onto serving dish and remove from pan. Carefully remove plastic wrap. Cover sides of torta with candied hazelnuts; sprinkle top with remaining chocolate. Cover and refrigerate until ready to serve. Serve with chocolate cookies or biscotti.

RIGHT: A decidedly decadent dessert, the Tiramisu Torta is a most pleasing marriage of tempting tastes. Creamier than butter, mascarpone cheese is Italian in origin. Nevertheless, its name is said to come from the Spanish *mas que bueno*, meaning "better than good."

Tiramisu Torta

Kim Stanford

flower swap
For the Garden Club

To kick off the start of summer, invite your fellow flora enthusiasts to put aside their gardening gloves and watering cans long enough to enjoy a fun-filled party guaranteed to please those with the greenest of thumbs.

Donning a wide-brimmed hat, planting tidy rows of seeds, carefully watering each one from day to day, then watching as the tiny plants burst from the soil and grow and grow—such are the pleasures in which the gardener indulges. For those who cherish this pastime, a weekly meeting with others bearing the same sentiments is eagerly awaited, especially in the summertime when there are plenty of crops and seedlings to share.

Inspired by this idea, a flower swap brings the group together for a splendid afternoon that's full of surprises. Miniature watering cans, rakes, and shovels peeking from the table's centerpiece of various greens draw guests near for a closer look. Pottery made from Mississippi clay provides an appropriate earthy look. Dragonfly napkin rings also serve as eye-catching accents to this setting that pays homage to the simple blessings of a day outdoors.

Causing additional burgeoning delight, a menu containing creative combinations results in countless compliments to the chef. Selections such as Sunflower Seed Muffins and Lavender Shortcakes sprout satisfied expressions, and the festivities conclude with the swapping of garden clippings, which leads to one conclusion: The good times will keep on growing.

Kim Stanford

Start a growing sensation among garden enthusiasts with a themed luncheon that's absolutely budding with opportunities for your creativity to blossom.

Cropping up here and there throughout this event, you'll find eensy weensy touches to tickle the fancies of fellow gardeners. Understated yet significant details are important to this table setting that illustrates the simplicity and beauty of a casual table.

Visions of neatly planted rows brimming with seedlings inspire the cheerful chromatic scheme. Watermelon green and ripe-tomato red jovially color the setting in the form of striped placemats, bold linens, and gerbera daisies. A few fresh ideas paired with an unbeatable menu provide the basis for this gathering, but the fun doesn't stop there . . .

Flower Swap

Clippings and cuttings straight from the garden make this an eagerly anticipated event. The only requirement is that each guest bring something to share, and when the group has finished lunching, each club member gets to return home with a new bit of green to begin growing in her own patch of land. Drawing names or numbers will help organize the process of swapping, but no matter how you choose to handle the exchange, the flower of friendship will undoubtedly be in full bloom. At the end of the day, give each guest an additional surprise—potted herbs tied with pretty bows, just another bit of green to grow and cherish.

Menu

Blackberry Lemon Tea

Fresh Broccoli Salad

Vegetable Ribbons

*Chicken Fettuccine with Smoked
Gouda Cream Sauce*

Sunflower Seed Muffins

*Lavender Shortcakes
with Strawberries and Cream*

Rosewater Cosmopolitan

Take the garden theme a step further with playful garnishes. Try accenting the Sunflower Seed Muffins with actual sunflowers or topping the Fresh Broccoli Salad with an easy-to-make tomato rose.

Blackberry Lemon Tea
Makes about 1 gallon

3¹/₂ quarts water, divided
3 family-size tea bags
1 cup sugar
³/₄ cup blackberry syrup
1 (12-ounce) can frozen lemonade concentrate, thawed

■ In a small sauce pan, boil 2 cups water over high heat. Remove from heat, add tea bags, cover and steep for 5 minutes; remove tea bags. In a large pitcher, combine tea, sugar, and blackberry syrup and stir until dissolved. Add lemonade concentrate and stir to mix well. Add remaining 3 quarts of water; stir to combine. Chill until ready to serve.

Fresh Broccoli Salad

step by step
Tomato Rose

Step 1. Select a medium-size tomato. Using a sharp paring knife, carefully cut the bottom of the tomato to form a thin base.

Step 2. Continue peeling the tomato in a long, thin strip to desired length. *Note: The longer the strip, the more layers of petals in the rose.*

Step 3. Tightly curl the strip, fleshy side inward, towards the base to form petals.

Step 4. As you approach the base, allow petals to become looser. Rest the finished curl on the base. Adjust petals slightly, if desired.

Fresh Broccoli Salad
Makes 8 servings

4 cups broccoli florets
3 cups cauliflower florets
1 (8-ounce) container sliced fresh mushrooms
2 cups halved grape tomatoes
1 cup chopped green olives
1 shallot, minced
¹/₃ cup fresh lemon juice
¹/₄ cup grated Parmesan cheese
2 teaspoons Dijon mustard
1 clove garlic, minced
¹/₄ teaspoon salt
¹/₈ teaspoon ground black pepper
¹/₂ cup vegetable oil

■ In a large bowl, combine broccoli, cauliflower, mushrooms, tomatoes, olives, and shallot; set aside. In work bowl of a food processor or container of a blender, combine lemon juice, cheese, mustard, garlic, salt, and pepper; process until smooth.
■ With processor or blender running, slowly pour in oil until well combined. Pour over salad and toss 1 hour before serving. Cover and chill.

Note: If more dressing is desired, double last seven ingredients of recipe.

Sunflower Seed Muffins

Sunflower Seed Muffins

Makes 1 dozen

1 cup all-purpose flour
1 cup whole-wheat flour
2¹/₂ teaspoons baking powder
¹/₂ teaspoon salt
¹/₂ cup dry-roasted sunflower kernels
1 large egg
³/₄ cup half-and-half
¹/₂ cup honey
¹/₄ cup buttermilk
¹/₄ cup unsalted butter, melted

■ Preheat oven to 375°. Grease a 12-count muffin tin; set aside.

■ In a medium bowl, combine flour, baking powder, and salt; stir to mix well. Stir in sunflower seeds. In a separate bowl, whisk together egg, half-and-half, honey, buttermilk, and butter. Combine flour mixture and egg mixture, stirring just until dry ingredients are moistened. Spoon batter into muffin cups, filling two-thirds full. Bake for 20 to 22 minutes.

RIGHT: Serve up heaping portions of delight with whimsical pewter utensils in the shape of a rake and shovel. Garden enthusiasts will love this subtle servingware as well as the vivid swirls and curls of delicious and nutritious Vegetable Ribbons.

Vegetable Ribbons

Chicken Fettuccine with Smoked Gouda Cream Sauce

Lavender Shortcakes with Strawberries and Cream

ABOVE: Strategically sprinkled garnishes add to the appeal of delicious dishes, such as the appetizing bits of pancetta atop Chicken Fettuccine with Smoked Gouda Cream Sauce. Fresh strawberry slices and dried lavender turn already taste-tempting lavender shortcakes into a sweetly sublime dessert.

Vegetable Ribbons
Makes 8 servings

6 large carrots, peeled
4 large zucchini squash
4 large yellow squash
2 bunches green onions
4 tablespoons butter
2 tablespoons extra virgin olive oil
2 tablespoons fresh thyme leaves
¹/₂ teaspoon salt
¹/₂ teaspoon ground black pepper

■ In a medium bowl, cut thin ribbons of carrots, zucchini, and yellow squash with a vegetable peeler; set aside. Cut green tops from green onions, discarding the bottoms.
■ In a large sauté pan, heat butter and oil over medium-high heat. Add vegetables and sauté for approximately 5 to 10 minutes until vegetables are tender. Stir in thyme, salt, and pepper. Cook 1 minute; serve immediately.

Chicken Fettuccine with Smoked Gouda Cream Sauce
Makes 8 servings

1 tablespoon olive oil
³/₄ cup chopped pancetta or 1 (3-ounce) package pancetta, chopped
¹/₂ cup butter
2 cups heavy whipping cream
1 large egg
¹/₂ teaspoon ground white pepper
¹/₂ teaspoon sugar
8 ounces smoked Gouda cheese, grated
1 (1-pound) box fettuccine noodles, cooked and drained
4 (6-ounce) packages or 24 ounces pre-cooked grilled chicken pieces

■ In a large sauté pan, heat oil over medium heat. Sauté pancetta until crispy; remove from pan, leaving drippings in pan. Reduce heat to medium-low and add butter, stirring until butter is melted.
■ In a medium bowl, whisk together cream, egg, pepper, and sugar; pour into sauté pan. Bring to a simmer and cook, stirring frequently, for 3 minutes. Remove from heat, and stir in cheese until melted.

■ In a microwave-safe bowl, heat chicken on High (100 percent power) until warm, about 2 minutes. To serve, place chicken on pasta and top with sauce. Garnish with pancetta.

Lavender Shortcakes with Strawberries and Cream
Makes about 1 dozen

3 cups sliced fresh strawberries
1 tablespoon sugar
2 cups all-purpose flour
¹/₂ cup sugar
2 tablespoons dried lavender
2 teaspoons baking powder
¹/₄ teaspoon baking soda
¹/₂ cup unsalted butter, softened
¹/₂ cup buttermilk
¹/₄ cup heavy whipping cream
1 teaspoon vanilla extract
1 cup heavy whipping cream
¹/₄ cup confectioners' sugar
1 egg white, lightly beaten
2 tablespoons coarse sugar

■ Preheat oven to 400°. Line a baking sheet with parchment paper; set aside.
■ In a medium bowl, combine strawberries and 1 tablespoon sugar. Cover and refrigerate.
■ In a medium bowl, combine flour, sugar, dried lavender, baking powder, and baking soda; stir to mix well. With a pastry knife or fork, cut butter into flour mixture until it resembles coarse crumbs. In a separate bowl, combine buttermilk, cream, and vanilla. Add buttermilk mixture to flour mixture, and stir until dough is just combined; dough will be sticky.
■ On a lightly floured surface, roll dough into a circle 1-inch in thickness. Cut with a 2¹/₂-inch cutter and place on prepared baking sheet. Brush with egg white and sprinkle with coarse sugar; bake for 12 to 14 minutes or until lightly browned. Remove to wire rack and cool completely.
■ In a medium bowl, combine remaining cream and confectioners' sugar. Beat with an electric mixer at medium speed until stiff peaks form.
■ To serve, split shortcakes in half horizontally. Layer strawberries and whipped cream on bottom halves; replace tops of shortcakes.
■ Garnish with a dollop of whipped cream, fresh strawberry slices, and dried lavender.

Sophisticated and feminine, innovative Rose Water Cosmopolitans were created with ladies in mind. With a scent as sweet as a garden of roses and a taste as smooth and refreshing as petals in the morning dew, this creative cocktail will earn instant approval. Roll the rim of each glass in colored sugar—matching pink is our favorite—and once the drink is poured, garnish with a tiny tea rose, just for decoration.

Rose Water Cosmopolitans
Makes 1 drink

2 ounces cranberry juice
1¼ ounces vodka
½ ounce Simple Syrup (recipe follows)
1 teaspoon fresh lime juice
¼ teaspoon rose water
Garnish: pink tea rose

■ Coat the rim of a chilled cocktail glass with pink sugar. Fill a shaker halfway with ice cubes. Add cranberry juice, vodka, Simple Syrup, lime juice, and rose water to the shaker.
■ Shake mixture vigorously for 5 to 10 seconds. Strain mixture into chilled cocktail glass. Garnish with a tea rose, if desired.

Simple Syrup:
Makes 1½ cups

1 cup sugar
1 cup water

■ In a small saucepan, combine sugar and water over medium-high heat, stirring constantly. Bring mixture to a boil; reduce heat to low and simmer 3 to 4 minutes, stirring constantly until sugar is dissolved.
■ Remove from heat and cool completely. Pour into an air-tight container. Store syrup in refrigerator for up to 3 weeks.

Rosewater Cosmopolitan

fairytale birthday
Wings & Whimsy

Candy-coated daydreams and fluttering butterfly wings—that's what little girls love. Drift away into a land of fairy tales and make-believe where each and every princess gets to become part of a special birthday wish.

With a dash of imagination and a sprinkle of pixie dust, you can transform an ordinary backyard into a magical land where birthday dreams come true. Streaming ribbons and glittering tutus bring to life fantasies of far-away castles and fairy princesses as young birthday guests enter a world of possibilities.

Gleeful giggles fill the air as the little ladies twist and twirl in ballerina fashion, waving glittering wands overhead. Flower garlands top their curly locks, leaving a sweet perfume in their wake as they cross the grassy lawn to the breathtaking centerpiece: a rainbow tower.

Yards of ribbons flow down from a crown of beautiful blossoms, and once each princess chooses a favorite color, the frolicking begins. Dancing 'round and 'round, the girls weave in and out in a kaleidoscope display.

After such enchanted exploits, the tiny highnesses are escorted to their royal court where light refreshments are served. Miniature tea sets and whimsical dishes add to the charm of this unforgettable event, and an artfully sculpted layered confection provides the literal icing on the cake for this event that is sure to evoke sparkling memories for years to come.

Ring around the roses, pocket full of posies—spinning, twirling, and whirling around a rainbow tower while holding a ribbon that shimmers in the sun is such fun!

Situated in the grassy clearing, an oh-so-tall rainbow tower with brightly colored streamers invites the young party guests to come and play. This festive focal point, fashioned at the top with spools and spools of sheer and satin ribbon, needs a sturdy and secure base so little ones can prance and dance around and around without a care.

Free-spirited games and giggles effortlessly weave their way into the afternoon activities centered around this fantastic display. In the middle of it all, a breathtaking bouquet of flowers sits atop the tower, cheerfully overseeing the tots and their merrymaking.

Flora and Fauna

The centerpiece to this fluttering affair, a spectacular four-layer cake from the bakery, garners interest from one and all. An ode to flora and fauna, tiny petals and butterflies made from fondant seem to flit and float on each tier of this confectionary masterpiece. To further satisfy the sweet tooth, a plateful of deliciously decorated sugar cookies acts as a dainty and delightful side dish. Served in whimsical ceramic dishes, these crumbly yummies look too pretty to eat—well, almost.

Entertaining Touches

Sparkling accents and glittering details create the wonderment of this wistful and wish-filled birthday party. Larger-than-life-sized posies placed in happily hued containers prove exceptionally pretty, and a gigantic cup-shaped punch bowl gives thirsty princesses the impression that they are in a pint-sized pixie paradise. Tied together with a shimmering bow, a bag of to-go goodies—dubbed Pixie Dust Snack Mix—allows the girls to take home a bit of the magic they've enjoyed throughout the afternoon.

Cranberry Apple Lemonade
Makes about 1 gallon

4 cups cranberry juice
2 cups apple juice
1 (12-ounce) container frozen lemonade
   concentrate, thawed
1 (2-liter) bottle ginger ale, chilled
Sliced lemons and limes

■ In a large container, combine cranberry juice, apple juice, and lemonade concentrate. Stir in ginger ale just before serving. Garnish with sliced lemons and limes.

Pixie Dust Snack Mix
Makes 3½ quarts

1 (11-ounce) box bug-shaped cinnamon graham
   crackers
1 (9-ounce) bag small pretzels
4 cups salted popped corn
3 cups pastel-colored jellybeans
2 cups frosted Cheerios®
2 cups fish-shaped cheese crackers

■ In a large bowl, combine all ingredients, tossing gently to combine.

Cranberry Apple Lemonade

Pixie Dust Snack Mix

Bacon-Wrapped Chicken Nuggets

Bacon-Wrapped Chicken Nuggets
Makes 4 dozen

1¹/₂ **pounds boneless, skinless chicken breasts**
¹/₄ **cup vegetable oil**
¹/₄ **cup soy sauce**
¹/₄ **cup honey**
1 **(16-ounce) package bacon, cut in thirds crosswise**
Honey Mustard Sauce (recipe follows)

■ Cut chicken into ¹/₂-inch chunks. Place chicken in a shallow dish or a resealable plastic bag.
■ In a small bowl, combine oil, soy sauce, and honey. Pour over chicken. Cover or seal, and marinate in refrigerator 4 hours to overnight. Drain chicken, and discard marinade.
■ Preheat oven to 350°. Wrap each piece of chicken with 1 piece bacon; skewer with toothpicks.
■ Place chicken on a lightly greased rack of a broiler pan. Bake 30 minutes, or until bacon is crisp. Serve with Honey Mustard Sauce.

Honey Mustard Sauce:
Makes 1²/₃ cups

1 **cup mayonnaise**
¹/₃ **cup prepared mustard**
¹/₃ **cup honey**

■ Combine all ingredients in a small bowl; cover and refrigerate.

RIGHT: Like walking into a daydream, an imaginative world emerges from a compilation of creativity and color. No need to match patterns and prints—the more eclectic the collection of dishes and linens, the better. Varying heights and sizes of serving pieces also lend themselves to this look, resulting in a party setting fit for fairies.

Ham and Cheese Phyllo Cups

Pink Sparkly Marshmallows

Pink Meringues with Sweetened Whipped Cream and Chocolate Butterflies

ABOVE: Some snacks, such as Ham and Cheese Phyllo Cups, will suit both the petite partygoers and their chaperones, but it's likely that Pink Sparkly Marshmallows—shining so sweetly with what appears to be fairy dust—will be the first treat to attract the hungry little ladies.

RIGHT: Melted chocolate becomes artfully enchanting in the shape of tiny butterflies. Surprisingly easy to make, these itty-bitty creations become the perfect toppers for Pink Meringues.

Ham and Cheese Phyllo Cups
Makes 45

3 (2.1-ounce) boxes frozen phyllo cups, thawed
1 (8-ounce) package cream cheese, softened
1½ cups shredded sharp Cheddar cheese
1½ cups shredded Mozzarella cheese
¾ cups chopped deli ham
¾ cups chopped deli turkey
Garnish: chopped fresh parsley

■ Preheat oven to 350°.
■ Place phyllo cups on a baking sheet; set aside.
■ In a medium bowl, combine cream cheese, shredded cheeses, ham, and turkey. Spoon mixture evenly into phyllo cups. Bake 12 to 15 minutes or until cheeses are melted. Sprinkle with chopped fresh parsley, if desired.

Fluffy Fairytale Fruit Dip
Makes 4 cups

1 (10-ounce) package frozen sliced strawberries, thawed
1 (8-ounce) package cream cheese, softened
1 (8-ounce) container strawberry flavored yogurt
1 (8-ounce) container frozen whipped topping, thawed
Pink Sparkly Marshmallows and whole strawberries for dipping

■ In the container of a food processor, combine all ingredients. Pulse until smooth. Cover and refrigerate. Serve with Pink Sparkly Marshmallows and strawberries.

Pink Meringues with Sweetened Whipped Cream and Chocolate Butterflies
Makes 3 dozen

3 egg whites, room temperature
¼ teaspoon cream of tartar
½ cup sugar
¼ teaspoon strawberry extract
3 drops red food coloring
2 cups heavy whipping cream
½ cup confectioners' sugar
Chocolate Butterflies (recipe follows)

■ In a large bowl, combine egg whites and cream of tartar. Beat with an electric mixer at medium-high speed until foamy. Gradually add sugar, 1 tablespoon at a time, beating until stiff peaks form. Fold in extract and food coloring.
■ Preheat oven to 250°. Spoon or pipe meringues into 1-inch mounds on parchment-lined baking sheets. Make a small indentation in center of each mound with the back of a spoon. Bake 30 minutes; turn oven off, and let sit in the oven 1 hour without opening the oven door. Let cool completely on baking sheets.
■ In a medium bowl, beat cream with an electric mixer until foamy. Gradually add sugar, beating until stiff peaks form. Spoon or pipe cream into indentations on meringues. Top cream with chocolate butterflies.

Chocolate Butterflies:
Makes a flock

1 (24-ounce) package chocolate confectioners' coating, melted

■ Spoon melted chocolate into a resealable plastic bag. Cut a small hole in one corner of the bag. Pipe 1 side of a butterfly-shaped wing onto parchment-lined baking sheets. Pipe an identical wing next to it, but not touching. Let chocolate cool.
■ Make V-shaped molds with heavy-duty aluminum foil. Place 1 wing on each side of V, with the center of wings touching. Pipe a line of chocolate to make the body of the butterfly, attaching the 2 wing pieces. Pipe antennaes on butterfly. Let cool. Store butterflies in a cool place until ready to serve.

Pink Sparkly Marshmallows
Makes about 40

1 (16-ounce) package large marshmallows
Shimmer dust (available at craft and cake stores)

■ Roll whole marshmallows in shimmer dust. Store tightly covered.

Curious Confections

Just right for little hands and mouths, cupcakes only add to the sweet sensations on this exciting occasion. On top of a layer of frosting, a bright blossom or butterfly design becomes the middle section of this extraordinary confection. A teeny tiny, completely edible cupcake is the next addition, which contains the finishing touch: a bold and skinny candle that soars high into the sky. What a treat!

Butterfly Sugar Cookies

Makes 2¹/₂ dozen

1 cup butter, softened
1 cup sugar
1 cup confectioners' sugar
2 large eggs
1 teaspoon almond extract
3¹/₂ cups all-purpose flour
¹/₂ teaspoon salt
¹/₄ teaspoon baking powder
Meringue Powder Icing (recipe follows)

■ In a large bowl, beat butter and sugars with an electric mixer until creamy. Beat in eggs and almond extract until fluffy.

■ In a small bowl, combine flour, salt, and baking powder. Gradually add to sugar mixture, beating until combined. Cover, and refrigerate 1 hour.

■ Preheat oven to 350°. On a lightly floured surface, roll dough to ¹/₄-inch thickness. Cut with butterfly-shaped cutters. Place on lightly greased cookie sheets, and bake 10 minutes or until edges are lightly browned.

■ Let cool on pans 2 minutes; remove to wire racks to cool completely. Paint with Meringue Powder Icing, if desired.

Meringue Powder Icing:

Makes 2¹/₂ cups

¹/₄ cup cold water
3 tablespoons meringue powder
2 cups confectioners' sugar
Food Colorings

■ In a medium bowl, beat water and meringue powder with a wire whisk until frothy. Whisk in confectioners' sugar until smooth. Whisk in food coloring, if desired.

■ Paint cookies using small pastry brushes. Pipe outlines and polka dots.

RIGHT: When preparing Butterfly Sugar Cookies, mix the icing colors to match your party decorations by adding various amounts and hues of food coloring. Be sure to start with just a few drops and then add accordingly until you reach the desired shade.

Butterfly Sugar Cookies

silver settings Luncheon for the Ladies

When hosting a group of ladies so dear, the occasion calls for something special. A silver spectacular, showcasing all of your polished pieces, sets the tone for this bright and shining celebration of friendship.

Crisp linens, fragrant flowers, and a plethora of silver; everything placed just-so. Pretty as can be, the dining room looks particularly pleasing today as light floods through the windows, filling the entire area with a sparkling radiance. Soon, the doorbell chimes like a herald announcing the arrival of your first guest.

One by one, they come, these women who have made such a difference in your life. Today, you honor them with a tangible example of appreciation in the form of a ladies' luncheon.

Hand-embroidered tablecloths with scalloped edges, heirloom china trimmed in platinum, and vibrant blossoms bearing the colors of springtime—touches of femininity create the look of this most anticipated mid-day meal. While guests dine on light and delicious fare, stories from the past come to life once more, affirming the constant and unbreakable bonds of the sisterhood shared among those seated together.

The dialogue continues long after the last scrumptious bite has been taken, and the ladies agree that this day has been most pleasant. To each, you present a silver tussie-mussie filled with flowers, a small token of thanks from a grateful heart.

Set the table with gleaming silver pieces that are as enduring as the companionship that surrounds this special day.

These wonderful women seated around the table have been at your side for all of the important events—and everyday moments—of your life. You want everything to be perfect on this day dedicated to showing them how much they mean to you. Buff the silver until it softly glows, each teaspoon, every goblet, the monogrammed tea service passed down from Grandmother's collection. Let them reflect the attention to detail that this occasion merits.

Create a centerpiece of flowers that reminds you of these special guests: the blue hydrangea from your best friend's wedding, pink roses your mother sent at your daughter's birth, hyacinths that grew in Aunt Dorothy's backyard, and calla lilies that are your sister's signature bloom. To further grace the table, slip a few nostalgic blossoms into tussie-mussies that have long been symbols of femininity.

Menu

Creamy Tomato Dill Soup

Parmesan Herb Rolls

Cucumber Salad

Cheesy Chicken and Asparagus Quiche

Raspberry Mousse

Peach Melba

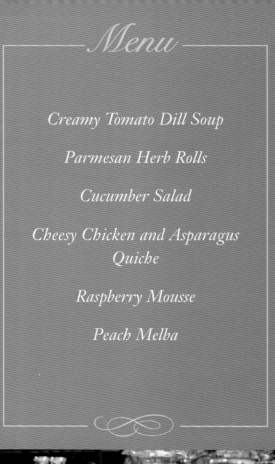

Creamy Tomato Dill Soup

Parmesan Herb Rolls

Creamy Tomato Dill Soup
Makes about 2 quarts

2 tablespoons olive oil
1 onion, finely chopped
3 cloves garlic, minced
4 cups chicken broth
1 (28-ounce) can crushed tomatoes
1 (6-ounce) can tomato paste
2 tablespoons sugar
3/4 teaspoon salt
1/4 teaspoon ground black pepper
1/2 cup heavy whipping cream
1/4 cup chopped fresh dill

■ In a Dutch oven, heat olive oil over medium heat. Add onion and sauté 4 to 5 minutes. Add garlic and sauté 1 minute.
■ Add chicken broth, crushed tomatoes, tomato paste, sugar, salt, and pepper. Bring to a boil; reduce heat and simmer 10 minutes. Stir in cream and dill. Bring to a simmer for 1 minute.

Parmesan Herb Rolls
Makes 1 dozen

1 cup grated Parmesan cheese
1 teaspoon dried minced onion
1 teaspoon dried oregano
1 teaspoon dried tarragon
1 teaspoon garlic salt
1 package frozen yeast bread dough, thawed
1/2 cup unsalted butter, melted

■ Grease a 12-cup muffin tin; set aside.
■ In a small bowl, combine Parmesan cheese, onion, oregano, tarragon, and garlic salt; set aside. Cut 36 (1-inch) pieces of dough. Roll each piece of dough in melted butter and then in cheese mixture. Place three balls into each muffin cup. Cover, and let rise in a warm place, free from drafts, until doubled in bulk, for approximately 2 hours.
■ Preheat oven to 375°. Bake 12 to15 minutes, or until golden brown.

Entertaining Touches

In planning a luncheon menu, choose foods considered to be of lighter fare. Begin with a soup course, and then introduce a selection of salads followed by sandwiches or slices of quiche. To save on time, use a frozen dough, which can be made into mouthwatering rolls by adding selected spices and Parmesan cheese. Finally, impress without stress by preparing an easy and elegant raspberry dessert.

Cucumber Salad with Cheesy Chicken and Asparagus Quiche

Raspberry Mousse

Cucumber Salad
Makes 6 to 8 servings

2 seedless cucumbers, sliced
2 shallots, peeled and thinly sliced
1/3 cup sour cream
6 tablespoons heavy whipping cream
3 teaspoons white balsamic vinegar
1 teaspoon Dijon mustard
1/2 teaspoon salt
1/4 teaspoon ground black pepper
1/4 teaspoon sugar
Garnish: chopped fresh parsley, chopped fresh chives

■ In a medium bowl, combine cucumbers and shallot. In a separate bowl, combine sour cream, cream, vinegar, mustard, salt, pepper, and sugar; stir to mix well. Combine sour cream mixture with cucumber mixture. Cover and chill.

Cheesy Chicken and Asparagus Quiche
Makes 6 servings

1/2 (15-ounce) package refrigerated piecrust (1 sheet)
2 tablespoons butter
2 tablespoons olive oil
3 cloves garlic, minced
1 cup chopped onion
1 cup chopped fresh asparagus (1-inch pieces)
2 boneless, skinless chicken breasts, diced (about 2 cups raw)
3 large eggs
1 cup half-and-half
1 teaspoon dry mustard
1/2 teaspoon salt
1/4 teaspoon black pepper
1 1/2 cups grated Monterey Jack cheese

■ Preheat oven to 450°.
■ Unroll piecrust on a lightly floured surface. Roll into a 12-inch circle. Place in a deep-dish 9-inch pie plate; fold edges under and crimp. Prick bottom and sides of piecrust with a fork. Bake 6 to 8 minutes.
■ Reduce heat to 375°.
■ In a large skillet, melt butter and olive oil over medium-high heat. Sauté garlic, onion, and asparagus 3 to 5 minutes, or until tender. With a slotted spoon, remove vegetables to another bowl, leaving as much oil in pan as possible.

■ Add chicken to pan and cook 5 to 7 minutes, or until lightly browned; remove from pan and set aside.
■ In a small bowl, whisk together eggs, half-and-half, mustard, salt, and pepper.
■ To assemble quiche, sprinkle 1 cup cheese over bottom of prepared crust. Layer chicken and vegetable mixture on top of cheese. Pour egg mixture over chicken and vegetables.
■ Top with remaining 1/2 cup cheese. Bake 30 to 35 minutes, or until set. Let quiche cool for 10 to 15 minutes before serving.

Raspberry Mousse
Makes 6 to 8 servings

3 tablespoons cold water
2 teaspoons unflavored gelatin
1 (8-ounce) package cream cheese, softened
1 cup confectioners' sugar
1/2 cup melted seedless raspberry preserves
1/4 cup unsalted butter, softened
2 cups heavy whipping cream
1 tablespoon sugar
Garnish: fresh raspberries

■ In a small microwave-safe bowl, combine water and gelatin; let stand 1 minute. Microwave on High power (100 percent) 1 minute, until gelatin is dissolved; set aside.
■ In a medium mixing bowl, combine cream cheese, confectioners' sugar, raspberry preserves, and butter. Beat with an electric mixer at medium speed until creamy; set aside.
■ In a separate bowl, beat cream and sugar until soft peaks form. Beat in dissolved gelatin until stiff peaks form. Fold together the cream cheese mixture and the whipped cream mixture until well combined. Garnish with fresh raspberries, if desired.

Peach Melba
Makes 6 servings

1 recipe Raspberry Syrup (recipe follows)
6 fresh peaches
1 pint fresh raspberries
Garnish: fresh mint leaves

Peach Melba

Entertaining with Ease

Peach Melba can be prepared in a variety of ways, but our version is unbelievably easy to make. As an additional timesaver, you can even substitute store-bought raspberry syrup. Just remember, fresh, ripe peaches are the secret to this dessert's success.

■ Prepare Raspberry Syrup; set aside.
■ Cut peaches in half, and remove pits.
■ To serve, place peach halves in serving dish. Top with fresh raspberries and Raspberry Syrup. Garnish with fresh mint, if desired.

Raspberry Syrup:
Makes about 1 1/2 cups

1 cup fresh or frozen raspberries
1/2 cup light corn syrup
1/4 cup sugar

■ In a small saucepan, combine raspberries, corn syrup, and sugar; bring to a boil, stirring frequently.
■ Reduce heat to low and simmer 10 minutes. Remove from heat, and press through a fine-mesh strainer, discarding solids.

sea & shore
Best of the Beach

Millions of grains of sand bordered by waters of sapphire blue and emerald green—side by side, these majestic marvels create a coastal escape that serves as the inspiration for a casual dinner featuring oceanic offerings.

A walk along the beach results in the discovery of countless tiny treasures, delicate shells washed ashore amid the frothy sea foam of rolling waves. These nautical finds quickly and easily turn into whimsical touches for the evening's seaside table setting.

Guests arrive in true relaxed style, preceded by the familiar sound of *flip-flop, flip-flop.* As a few gulls chime in with a *caw* or two, the ocean continues to sing her rhythmic song of ebb and flow, a steady symphony of the sea.

The sun begins to sink into the horizon, almost melting away in the distance with streams of light dancing across the water, and soon, the golden glow shifts from the setting sun to the conversation around the table.

The happy chatter turns to choruses of oohs and aahs as you present fresh shrimp, scallops, oysters, and pan-fried snapper—the best of the beach. Scrumptious sides accompany these tasty temptations, and Key Lime Parfaits end the feasting in the sweetest way. Goblets of sangria clink in glad accord as all agree to stay a while longer, lounging and laughing by the sea.

Ocean Gems

While the waves tumble playfully upon the shore, scoop up a handful of silvery sand and see what precious treasures from the briny blue are revealed. Shells with their curves and swirls, spots and dots provide an ocean of possibilities for an evening of entertaining.

Calming Colors

Replicate the serene coloring of the sea with nautical-hued table settings. Pair crisp white linen napkins with others in the azure blue of an endless summer sky. Like jewels from the ocean floor, iridescent marbles combine with rock salt to make a shimmering bed for oysters on the half shell.

Night Lights

Capture a bit of sand and sea in a clear glass container. This miniature ocean becomes a base to hold a pristine pillar candle. Position a candle at each place setting, and after dinner, allow each guest to take home the lovely reminder of the seaside gathering.

Sea & Shore: Best of the Beach 107

Menu

White Peach Sangria

Shrimp and Corn Bisque

Crab Salad in Artichoke Hearts

Pan-Fried Snapper with Brown Butter

Parmesan Creamed Spinach

Wild Rice Pilaf

Sea Scallops with Tomato Beurre Blanc

Key Lime Parfaits

White Peach Sangria
Makes about 3 quarts

2 (750-ml) bottles pinot grigio or dry white wine
1¹/₂ cups peach schnapps
2 (11.3-ounce) cans peach nectar
1 cup frozen pink lemonade concentrate, thawed
¹/₂ cup sugar
1 cup frozen sliced peaches
1 cup frozen raspberries

■ In a large pitcher, combine wine, peach schnapps, peach nectar, lemonade concentrate, and sugar. Stir until sugar dissolves. Add peaches and raspberries; chill for 2 hours. Serve chilled or over ice.

White Peach Sangria

Shrimp and Corn Bisque
Makes 2¹/₂ quarts

1¹/₂ pounds large shrimp
¹/₄ cup plus 2 tablespoons olive oil
1¹/₂ cups chopped onion
³/₄ cup chopped carrot
³/₄ cup chopped celery
1 tablespoon salt
³/₄ teaspoon ground black pepper
1 cup dry sherry
3 tablespoons tomato paste
3 garlic cloves, minced
2 quarts water
6 bay leaves
¹/₂ cup butter
¹/₂ cup flour
2 cups frozen cream-style corn
1 cup heavy whipping cream
Garnish: chopped fresh parsley

■ Peel and devein shrimp, reserving shells. Cover and refrigerate shrimp for later use.
■ In a Dutch oven, heat ¹/₄ cup oil over medium-high heat. Add shrimp shells; sauté 4 minutes. Add onion, carrot, celery, salt, and pepper; sauté 5 minutes. Add sherry; cook 2 minutes. Add tomato paste and garlic; cook 2 to 3 minutes, stirring frequently. Add water and bay leaves; bring to a boil. Reduce heat to medium-low and simmer 45 minutes. Strain shrimp broth, discarding solids; set aside.
■ In a Dutch oven, melt butter over medium heat. Add flour and cook 3 minutes, stirring constantly. Add corn and cook 3 to 4 minutes, stirring constantly. Gradually add shrimp broth, whisking constantly until smooth. Bring to a boil; reduce heat to medium-low and simmer for 20 minutes.
■ Add cream, whisking constantly until smooth; cook 2 minutes until just heated through.
■ In a large skillet, heat 2 tablespoons oil over medium-high heat. Add shrimp and sauté 2 to 3 minutes on each side, until shrimp turn pink. To serve, ladle bisque into bowls and garnish with sautéed shrimp and parsley, if desired.

Entertaining Touches

The key to this menu is starting with the freshest seafood possible. This is easy to achieve at the beach where fisherman proudly display the catch of the day at seafood markets, but when purchasing locally, seek out specialty markets and ask the purveyor about freshness if there is any question.

Shrimp and Corn Bisque

Pan-Fried Snapper with Brown Butter
Parmesan Creamed Spinach
Wild Rice Pilaf

Sea Scallops with Tomato Beurre Blanc

ABOVE: An entrée as delicious as Pan-Fried Snapper needs little garnish, so add a simple slice of lemon and a pinch of parsley. A scalloped half-shell dish on top of a pearly plate adds oceanic whimsy to the presentation of appetizing scallops.

RIGHT: Confetti-colored Crab Salad in Artichoke Hearts is the perfect way to begin this seaside dinner.

Crab Salad in Artichoke Hearts

Crab Salad in Artichoke Hearts
Makes 2 cups

1 (8-ounce) container crab meat, picked for shells
1/3 cup finely chopped red bell pepper
1/4 cup finely chopped green onion
2 tablespoons chopped fresh parsley
1/4 cup vegetable oil
2 tablespoons fresh lemon juice
2 tablespoons white balsamic vinegar
1/2 teaspoon lemon zest
1/4 teaspoon salt
1/8 teaspoon ground black pepper
2 (14-ounce) cans large artichoke hearts, drained

■ In a medium bowl, combine crab meat, red pepper, green onion, and parsley. In a small bowl, combine oil and next 5 ingredients, stirring to mix well.
■ Pour oil mixture over crab mixture, tossing gently to combine. Cover and chill 2 hours.
■ Trim bottom off each artichoke heart; cut in half lengthwise. Spoon crab salad onto each prepared artichoke heart.

Pan-Fried Snapper with Brown Butter
Makes 6 servings

1 cup flour
1/2 teaspoon salt
1/4 teaspoon ground black pepper
1 cup milk
1/2 cup olive oil
6 (6-ounce) snapper fillets
2 tablespoons fresh lemon juice
2 tablespoons chopped fresh parsley
1/4 cup butter
Garnish: lemon slices

■ In a shallow dish, combine flour, salt, and pepper. Pour milk into a separate shallow dish. In a 10-inch non-stick skillet, heat olive oil over medium-high heat.
■ Dip fish fillets in milk and dredge in flour mixture, shaking off excess. Sauté for 3 to 4 minutes on each side, until lightly browned and fish is tender. Sprinkle fish with lemon juice and parsley.
■ In a small saucepan, melt butter over medium heat; cook until lightly browned. Pour hot butter over fish. Garnish with lemon slices, if desired. Serve immediately.

Parmesan Creamed Spinach
Makes 6 to 8 servings

1/4 cup butter
1/4 cup flour
2 cloves garlic, minced
2 1/2 cups milk
1/2 cup heavy whipping cream
1/2 teaspoon salt
1/4 teaspoon ground white pepper
2 (1-pound) packages chopped frozen spinach, drained completely
1 cup freshly grated Parmesan cheese

■ In a Dutch oven, melt butter over medium heat. Whisk in flour and cook for 4 to 5 minutes. Stir in garlic; cook for 2 minutes. Gradually whisk in milk, cream, salt, and pepper. Whisking constantly, bring mixture to a simmer and cook 10 minutes until mixture thickens. Reduce heat to low.
■ Add spinach and cheese, stirring well to combine. Cook 2 minutes, stirring constantly.

Wild Rice Pilaf
Makes 6 to 8 servings

3 tablespoons butter
1/2 cup chopped onion
2 cups long-grain-and-wild-rice blend
1 quart hot chicken broth
1/2 teaspoon salt
1/4 teaspoon ground black pepper

■ Preheat oven to 350°.
■ In a Dutch oven, melt butter over medium heat. Add onion and sauté for 2 to 3 minutes, or until tender. Add rice and sauté 1 to 2 minutes, stirring constantly. Add hot chicken broth and bring to a boil; stir in salt and pepper. Cover and bake for 25 to 30 minutes, or until liquid is absorbed. Fluff with fork before serving.

Sea Scallops with Tomato Beurre Blanc
Makes 6 servings

2 tablespoons olive oil
12 large fresh sea scallops
1 recipe Tomato Beurre Blanc (recipe follows)

On the Side

Keep several dipping sauces handy for fresh shrimp. For a simple cocktail sauce, blend together ketchup, horseradish, and lemon juice, and enjoy!

■ In a large non-stick skillet, heat oil over medium-high heat. Add scallops; cook for 2 to 3 minutes on each side, until golden brown. Serve with Tomato Beurre Blanc.

Tomato Beurre Blanc:
Makes about 1 cup

1/4 cup dry white wine
1 tablespoon white wine vinegar
1 shallot, finely chopped
1/2 cup cold butter, cut into pieces
1 medium tomato, seeded and chopped
1/8 teaspoon salt
1/8 teaspoon ground black pepper

■ In a small saucepan, combine wine, vinegar, and shallot over medium-high heat. Bring to a simmer and cook for 2 to 3 minutes, until about 2 tablespoons of liquid remains.
■ Gradually whisk in butter. Remove from heat and whisk until smooth. Stir in tomato, salt, and pepper. Serve immediately.

Key Lime Parfaits
Makes 6 to 8 servings

Prepared or commercial angel food cake
2 (8-ounce) packages cream cheese, softened
1 cup confectioners' sugar
2 tablespoons key lime zest
2 teaspoons vanilla extract
1½ cups heavy whipping cream
1 recipe Key Lime Filling (recipe follows)

■ Cut angel food cake into 1-inch cubes; set aside. In a large mixing bowl, beat cream cheese, confectioners' sugar, lime zest, and vanilla at medium speed with an electric mixer until smooth. Add whipping cream and beat at high speed until soft peaks form. Cover and chill until ready to use.

■ To assemble, layer angel food cake, cream cheese mixture, and Key Lime Filling. Repeat layers as desired. Refrigerate until ready to serve.

Key Lime Filling:
Makes about 3½ cups

5 large egg yolks
¾ cup sugar
⅓ cup fresh key lime juice
1 tablespoon key lime zest
½ cup butter, cut into pieces
1 cup heavy whipping cream

■ In top of a double boiler, whisk together egg yolks, sugar, lime juice, and lime zest. Bring water to a boil, reduce heat, and cook over simmering water, whisking constantly for 6 to 8 minutes, until mixture thickens. Remove from heat and gradually whisk in butter; cool completely.

■ In a medium bowl, beat cream at medium speed with an electric mixer until soft peaks form. Gently fold cooled filling into whipped cream. Cover and chill until ready to use.

RIGHT: To finish with flair, serve frosty Key Lime Parfaits. Though available in abundance at the beach, key limes may be difficult to find locally; regular limes will serve as a suitable substitute in the creation of this delicious dish.

Key Lime Parfaits

well served
The Courtside Soiree

After a gentle toss into the air, a mighty swing sends the tiny green ball rocketing across the net. Returns and volleys lead to an intense match-up, but in the end, everyone wins with a sportsmanship-promoting after-party.

Fierce competition is expected out on the court. Power forehands and precision backhands coupled with fancy footwork and quick decision-making certainly make for an exciting morning of game play. Of course, after all that exercise a little rejuvenation is in high demand, and what better to feed the need than light and lively, sport-friendly fare.

Having worked up an appetite on the tennis court, players eye the nearby spread of bite-sized treats, but thirst quenchers come first: ice-cold water and tangy lemonade. Pretty tables dressed in cheerful colors encourage opponents to sit side by side, sharing in the charm of an inviting setting. Lovely dishes and dinnerware elevate the essence of patio-style elegance, and ruffled parrot tulips show off their blossoming beauty as an impressive yet simple centerpiece.

Exchanging stories and strategies, the athletes let their intensity for victory subside, and soon, each competitor begins to feel like part of this particularly pleasant team of friends. Munching on sugary Sunshine Cookies and trophy-worthy Banana Split Meringues, the group unanimously acknowledges the day's activities as an absolute triumph, a merited match-up that promises many a repeat.

The Pink of Perfection

Celebrate the setting of this party by adorning the table in the fresh colors of the great outdoors. Begin with a mix of pink linens in coordinating fabrics, then add mismatched dinnerware—perhaps Depression glass with hobnail trim or blossom-shaped ceramics—in the same roseate hues. The common color draws the pieces together for an eclectic blend of patterns and styles. A witty nod to the bouncing tennis ball, melon balls marinated in honey and basil and presented in morning glory-shaped crystal stemware serve as a clever and dainty starter to the non-competitive part of the gathering.

Serve Up Some Fun

A thoughtful hostess will include a little something extra for her guests to take home with them, a keepsake to remind them of the delightful time spent in the company of dear friends. Since this party sports a tennis theme, bright colors are in order. Wrap up individual lime-colored tennis balls in pale pink netting and tie with perky polka-dot grosgrain ribbon. Anything monogrammed is destined to be considered a crowd favorite, and a white tennis towel with initials embroidered in a vibrant shade is no exception. A double delight, these much-appreciated going-home goodies let the ladies know you're looking forward to a rousing rematch of the day's play.

Menu

Tennis Whites Pimento Cheese

Barbecue Chicken Salad in Tortilla Cups

Artichoke Parmesan Strudel

Banana Split Meringues

Frosty Lemonade Cookies

A lunchtime gathering at the tennis court should be casual, but that doesn't mean you have to sacrifice style. Quite the contrary! Begin by grouping cylindrical glass vases as a centerpiece and fill with stems of spring flowers, such as Rembrandt tulips, for a touch of elegance. Scrolled tiered serving trays mirror the curves of the tempered glass-top tables crafted in black wrought iron, and cheerful linens add just the right note of charm. Include menu items that are easy to eat, such as tea sandwiches and salads, so that guests have the freedom to move about and chat. After an active morning of volleys and lobs on the tennis court, the ladies will be grateful for a refreshing respite to rest and regroup.

Tennis Whites Pimento Cheese
Makes 3 cups

1 cup grated White Cheddar cheese
1 cup grated Monterey Jack cheese
1 cup grated Gruyère cheese
¹/₂ cup finely chopped pecans
1 cup mayonnaise
¹/₂ teaspoon ground black pepper
¹/₂ cup drained diced pimentos
1 loaf sourdough bread, crust removed

■ In a medium bowl, combine the cheeses and pecans. Stir in mayonnaise and pepper until well blended. Gently fold in pimentos. Cover and refrigerate.
■ To serve, spread on sourdough bread and cut into finger sandwiches.

Tennis Whites Pimento Cheese

ABOVE: For a delicious reinvention of an old luncheon favorite, serve Tennis Whites Pimento Cheese sandwiches. Heaped between slices of sourdough bread, this savory spread combines three white cheeses with pimentos and a sprinkling of chopped pecans for a true Southern touch.

Barbecue Chicken Salad in Tortilla Cups

ABOVE: This menu features dishes that are substantial enough to satisfy a player's appetite after a few sets on the court, but still light enough to allow her to return to play after lunch. Fill tortilla chip cups with Barbecue Chicken Salad for a flavor-blasted appetizer.

Barbecue Chicken Salad in Tortilla Cups
Makes 3¹/₂ cups

3 cups chopped cooked chicken
³/₄ cup drained black beans
³/₄ cup drained whole kernel yellow corn with red and green bell peppers*
¹/₄ cup finely chopped red onion
¹/₂ cup hickory smoke flavored barbecue sauce
¹/₄ cup mayonnaise
¹/₄ cup sour cream
¹/₄ teaspoon salt
¹/₄ teaspoon ground black pepper
Bowl-shaped tortilla chips**
Garnish: fresh cilantro

■ In a medium bowl, combine chicken, black beans, corn, and onion. In a separate bowl, combine barbecue sauce, mayonnaise, sour cream, salt, and pepper; stir to mix well. Combine chicken mixture and barbecue sauce mixture, stirring to mix well. Cover and refrigerate.
■ To serve, spoon chicken salad into tortilla chips and garnish with fresh cilantro. Refrigerate and reserve remaining chicken salad for another use.

*For testing purposes, we used Green Giant Mexicorn®.
**For testing purposes, we used Tostitos Scoops®.

Artichoke Parmesan Strudel

Banana Split Meringues

ABOVE: A versatile tidbit, Artichoke Parmesan Strudel is equally good served hot or at room temperature. A bit more finicky—but only due to the addition of fresh banana slices—are the scrumptious Banana Split Meringues, which hold a truly decadent surprise inside: chocolate chips.

RIGHT: Frosty Lemonade Cookies are made with a basic recipe that becomes extraordinary when frosted with creamy lemonade-flavored icing and sprinkled with brilliant yellow decorator sugar. Serve with a complementing beverage, such as your favorite homemade or instant lemonade.

Frosty Lemonade Cookies

Artichoke Parmesan Strudel
Makes about 2 dozen

1 (15-ounce) box frozen puff pastry, thawed
2 (8-ounce) packages cream cheese, softened
1¼ cups freshly grated Parmesan cheese, divided
5 large eggs, divided
¼ cup chopped fresh parsley
2 tablespoons fresh lemon juice
2 teaspoons dried thyme
¼ teaspoon salt
¼ teaspoon ground black pepper
2 (14-ounce) cans artichoke hearts, drained and chopped

■ Preheat oven to 400°. Grease a 13x9x2-inch pan; set aside.
■ On a lightly floured surface, roll each puff pastry sheet into a 10x14-inch rectangle. Place one sheet in bottom of prepared pan; prick bottom with fork. Bake for 8 minutes; set aside to cool slightly.
■ In a medium bowl, combine cream cheese, 1 cup Parmesan cheese, 4 eggs, parsley, lemon juice, thyme, salt, and pepper. Beat with an electric mixer at medium speed until smooth. Stir in artichokes until well combined.
■ Spread artichoke mixture on bottom crust in pan and top with remaining puff pastry sheet. Lightly beat remaining egg and gently brush on top of crust.
■ Bake for 15 minutes, sprinkle with remaining Parmesan cheese and bake for 10 to 12 minutes, until lightly browned. Cool for 10 minutes and cut into squares.

Banana Split Meringues
Makes 1 dozen

5 egg whites
½ teaspoon cream of tartar
⅔ cup sugar
½ cup semisweet miniature chocolate morsels
3 large bananas, sliced
¼ cup banana liqueur
2 (3.4-ounce) boxes banana cream instant pudding
2 cups heavy whipping cream
1 cup sour cream
½ cup milk

½ cup confectioners' sugar
¼ cup chopped hazelnuts
¼ cup chopped maraschino cherries
Garnish: chocolate syrup

■ Preheat oven to 300°. Line 2 baking sheets with parchment paper; set aside.
■ In a medium mixing bowl, combine egg whites and cream of tartar. Beat with an electric mixer at medium speed until soft peaks form. Gradually add sugar and beat until stiff peaks form and meringue is shiny in appearance; fold in chocolate morsels.
■ Spread meringue into 12 (3½-inch) circles on prepared baking sheets. Using the back of a spoon, make an indentation in the center of each meringue.
■ Bake on middle rack of oven for 25 to 30 minutes, or until lightly browned. Turn off heat and leave meringues in oven for 1 hour, or until completely dry. Remove to wire racks to cool completely.
■ In a small bowl, combine bananas and banana liqueur. Let stand 15 minutes; drain. In a large mixing bowl, combine pudding, cream, sour cream, milk, and confectioners' sugar. With an electric mixer, beat at medium speed until stiff peaks form. Spoon or pipe banana cream mixture into each meringue. Top each meringue with bananas, hazelnuts, cherries, and chocolate syrup.

Frosty Lemonade Cookies
Makes about 2½ dozen

1½ cups sugar
1 cup unsalted butter, softened
2 large eggs
1 tablespoon lemon zest
½ teaspoon lemon extract
4½ cups all-purpose flour
1 teaspoon baking powder
1 teaspoon baking soda
½ teaspoon salt
1 cup sour cream
1 recipe Lemonade Icing (recipe follows)
Garnish: yellow decorator sugar

■ In a large mixing bowl, combine sugar and butter. Beat at medium speed with an electric

mixer until fluffy. Add eggs, lemon zest, and lemon extract, beating well.
■ In a medium bowl, combine flour, baking powder, baking soda, and salt. Add to sugar mixture alternately with sour cream, beginning and ending with flour mixture. Beat at low speed, blending well after each addition.
■ Divide dough into thirds; wrap each portion in plastic wrap and refrigerate 2 hours.
■ Preheat oven to 400°. Line a baking sheet with parchment paper; set aside. On lightly floured surface, roll each portion of chilled dough to ¼-inch thickness. Cut out shapes with cookie cutters. Place on prepared baking sheet. Bake 6 to 8 minutes. Transfer to wire racks to cool.
■ Decorate with Lemonade Icing. Sprinkle with decorator sugar, if desired.

Lemonade Icing:
Makes about 2 cups

3 cups confectioners' sugar
6 tablespoons unsalted butter, softened
6 tablespoons frozen lemonade concentrate, thawed

■ In a medium bowl, combine sugar, butter, and lemonade concentrate. Beat with an electric mixer at low speed, until well combined.

open house
Warm Welcomes

When it's cold outside, kindle the embers of friendship with a jovial meet-and-greet for friends and neighbors. Trays of tantalizing appetizers also spark plenty of interest, spreading warmth and cheer to all who gather near.

Here the conversation is lively, the food is delicious, and the only things opened more than the front door are the hearts of the gracious hosts. Long-time friends and next-door neighbors all mix and mingle in this festive atmosphere.

New acquaintances are easily formed over a platter of Stuffed Mushrooms, which prompt guests to concur that these tiny caps full of Parmesan cheese and herbs may quite possibly be the best bite-sized food they've ever tasted—that is until they try the Mini Muffalettas. And then, of course, there are the Bacon-Wrapped Figs, which also happen to be part of a grand buffet that showcases an entire array of eye-catching, taste-tempting appetizers.

But that's not all. Mugs of rich Hot Chocolate Mocha and Apple Cider Tea take away any lingering signs of chill. Easy-to-make treats, in the form of S'more Brownies and Creamy Lemon Petit Fours, bring even more smiles. Requests for not only seconds but also recipes joyfully ring in the ears of the party's hosts, who enjoy the gathering so much that they begin planning their next Open House.

The personalized touch of a homemade invitation sets the tone for a peppy party and lets folks know they can expect a friendly hello when you greet them at the door.

MATERIALS YOU WILL NEED

- Ruler
- Pencil
- Assorted ribbons
- Hole punch
- Utility knife
- Tape or glue
- Colorful, patterned scrapbooking papers
- Heavy-duty card stock

step by step Easy Invitations

1

2

3

Step 1. Create a stiff card stock stencil out of a 6-inch square and 4 even semi-circles. Trace stencil with a pencil onto colored paper.

Step 2. Using a sharp utility knife, cautiously cut around the traced stencil. Flip cutout paper over and fold each semicircle inward along the sides of the original square, creating tight seams at the folds.

Step 3. Glue a pre-cut invitation into the square. Fold one pair of opposite flaps into the center. Punch a hole close to the edge of each side of the second pair of flaps, as shown. Fold these flaps inward and tie with ribbon.

Clever carryout boxes are such fun. For added class, consider crafting your own using colors and prints that complement your theme.

step by step
Creative Carton

Step 1. Begin with a clean to-go box, available at craft stores and local eateries. Unfold the box, flattening seams as shown.

Step 2. Protect your original box by creating a stencil traced onto stiff card stock. Using a sharp utility knife, cautiously cut around the stencil. Next, trace the stencil onto colored card stock.

Step 3. Once again, cut around new stencil. Fold each leaf toward the center, creating tight seams at the folds, and tuck small sides into large sides. Secure all interior flaps and wrap an accent ribbon around the carton, creating a homemade gift box suitable for any occasion.

Entertaining Touches

Break the ice and maximize the mingling by arranging food in stations throughout the house. Friends will flock to their favorite fare, sparking plenty of conversation between munches. Although most of these open-house appetizers work well as nibble-friendly finger foods, don't forget to provide appropriate dinnerware, serving spoons, and lots of napkins. Also, plan accordingly for foods best served hot—such as Shrimp and Mushroom Wontons.

Vegetable Dill Party Dip
Makes 2³/₄ cups

1 (16-ounce) carton sour cream
¹/₂ cup mayonnaise
¹/₄ cup finely chopped red bell pepper
¹/₄ cup finely chopped yellow bell pepper
2 tablespoons chopped fresh parsley
2 tablespoons minced onion
1 tablespoon chopped fresh dill
1 teaspoon dry mustard
1 teaspoon seasoned salt
¹/₂ teaspoon garlic powder

■ In a medium bowl, combine all ingredients; cover and chill 3 hours. Serve with crackers, bagel chips, or pretzel chips.

Vegetable Dill Party Dip

Apple Cider Tea
Makes 1 gallon

8 cups water
3 family-size tea bags
3 to 4 cinnamon sticks
1 lemon, sliced in thin slices
³/₄ cup sugar
¹/₂ gallon apple cider

■ Bring water, tea bags, cinnamon sticks, and lemon to a boil. Reduce heat and simmer for 20 minutes.
■ Remove tea bags, cinnamon sticks, and lemon; add sugar. Stir until sugar dissolves completely. Pour in apple cider and heat through. Serve hot or over ice.

Apple Cider Tea

Hot Chocolate Mocha
Makes 8 to 10 cups

6 tablespoons medium-roast ground coffee
8 cups (64-ounces) water
1 (14-ounce) can fat-free sweetened condensed milk
6 tablespoons Ghirardelli Sweet Ground
   Chocolate and Cocoa Powder
1 teaspoon vanilla extract

■ Brew coffee and water in a coffee maker. Pour brewed coffee into a large saucepan. Whisk in sweetened condensed milk, chocolate/cocoa powder, and vanilla extract. Keep warm on low heat.

Bacon–Wrapped Figs
Makes 2 dozen

24 dried figs, stems removed
8 slices bacon, sliced into thirds
¹/₂ cup soy sauce
2 tablespoons dark brown sugar
2 tablespoons fresh lemon juice

■ Preheat oven to 350°.
■ Wrap each fig with one-third slice bacon and secure with toothpick.
■ In a small bowl, mix together soy sauce, dark brown sugar, and lemon juice. Dip each bacon-wrapped fig into sauce, coating well.
■ Place on a sheet pan lined with aluminum foil and bake for 20 minutes, or until done. Serve warm.

Note: To help prevent the toothpicks from burning in the oven, soak them in water before skewering appetizers.

RIGHT: Warm up a cold day with Hot Chocolate Mocha. For those who prefer a stronger java flavor, prepare the coffeehouse-worthy blend with rounded tablespoons of a dark roast.

Hot Chocolate Mocha

Mini Muffalettas

Smoked Tuna and Cucumber Canapés

Bacon Wrapped Figs

ABOVE: The muffaletta originated at the beginning of the 20th century in a small shop in New Orleans, Louisiana. Described as one of the world's great sandwiches, a typical muffaletta, like our mini version, consists of bread, meats, cheeses, and the heart of the creation: olive salad. Canapés, consisting of creatively cut cucumbers bearing a creamy concoction of smoked tuna, are also an important part of this fun-filled assembly.

Mini Muffalettas
Makes about 3 dozen

1 loaf sourdough or white party bread, sliced
Butter or margarine
1½ pounds salami
1½ pounds Baby Swiss or Havarti cheese
1½ pounds ham (Mortadella, Prosciutto, Coppa)
1½ pounds Provolone cheese
1 recipe Olive Salad (recipe follows)

■ Spread thin layer of butter on each slice of party bread. Slice meat and cheeses into ¼-inch-thick small squares with a square cutter or a knife. Layer sliced salami, Baby Swiss or Havarti cheese, ham, and Provolone on bread.
■ Garnish with Olive Salad.

Olive Salad:
Makes 1 quart

2 cloves garlic, minced
1 cup chopped stuffed green olives
1 cup chopped black olives
1 (7-ounce) jar or ½ cup chopped roasted red peppers
1 tablespoon chopped capers, (rinse before chopping)
3 tablespoons chopped fresh parsley
¾ cup olive oil
2 tablespoons white-wine vinegar

■ In a medium bowl, mix together garlic, olives, peppers, capers, parsley, olive oil, and vinegar. Refrigerate for 12 to 24 hours. Keep refrigerated in air-tight container for up to 2 weeks.

Note: If you want additional Olive Salad on the Mini Muffalettas, spread a layer on top of the butter before layering the meats and cheeses.

Smoked Tuna and Cucumber Canapés
Makes about 3½ dozen

2 large cucumbers
2 (5-ounce) packages StarKist Hickory Smoked Tuna®
1 (8-ounce) package cream cheese, softened
1 teaspoon hot pepper sauce
½ cup chopped unsalted mixed nuts, toasted

2 tablespoons minced fresh parsley
½ teaspoon garlic salt
½ teaspoon black pepper
Garnish: paprika

■ Score cucumber with a channel knife and slice into ¼-inch slices.
■ In a small bowl, combine tuna, cream cheese, hot sauce, nuts, parsley, garlic salt, and black pepper. Pipe onto center of each cucumber. Sprinkle with paprika.

Shrimp and Mushroom Wontons
Makes 5 dozen

2 tablespoons butter
2 cloves of garlic, chopped
1 cup chopped fresh mushrooms
½ cup chopped green onion
2 teaspoons soy sauce
2 teaspoons toasted sesame oil
¼ teaspoon salt
¼ teaspoon black pepper
1 pound fresh shrimp, peeled, deveined, and chopped
60 wonton or pot sticker wrappers
Vegetable oil or peanut oil
1 recipe Soy-Sesame Dipping Sauce (recipe follows)

■ In a large skillet, melt butter over medium heat; add garlic, and cook 1 minute. Add mushrooms, and cook 4 to 5 minutes or until all liquid evaporates. Add green onion, and cook 2 minutes. Stir in soy sauce, sesame oil, salt, and pepper. Stir in shrimp, and cook, just until pink.
■ Spoon 2 teaspoons shrimp mixture onto center of each wonton wrapper. Moisten wrapper edges with water; bring corners together, pressing edges to seal.
■ In a Dutch oven, pour oil to a depth of 6 inches; heat to 350°. Fry wontons, in batches, 2 minutes on each side or until golden brown. Drain on paper towels. Serve warm.

Soy-Sesame Dipping Sauce:
Makes 1½ cups

⅔ cup soy sauce
½ cup rice vinegar

Shrimp and Mushroom Wontons

Flavorful Assortment

When entertaining, it is important to remember that everyone has different tastes in food. With a selection of recipes that represents an array of spices, sauces, and seasonings, guests should have no problems finding at least one item that suits their particular likings, ensuring the party will be filled with fun for each and every one!

4 teaspoons toasted sesame oil
4 teaspoons sugar
2 tablespoons fresh lemon juice
4 teaspoons Thai garlic chile pepper sauce (optional)
Garnish: sesame seeds and chopped scallions

■ In a small bowl, combine soy sauce, vinegar, oil, sugar, and lemon juice. If desired, add Thai garlic chile pepper sauce. Whisk to combine.
■ Garnish sauce with sesame seeds and chopped scallions.

Bright Idea

Mixing and mingling is the theme of the day, so don't be afraid to carry it out in your décor as well. Funky flowers and gem-studded candlesticks look right at home beside square platters and checkered mugs. Stripes, polka dots, and swirly-doos—popping patterns are welcomed sights as well, contributing to the fresh look fashioned for this indoor gathering. Pinks, greens, reds, and browns combine to create an ambiance that announces, "I'm glad you're here," even on the coldest of winter days. Settle in and chat it up. Everyone has a place in this tapestry of taste.

Stuffed Mushrooms
Makes 4 dozen

48 mushrooms (Baby Portabellas or Creminis)
1/4 cup butter, melted
3/4 cup grated Parmesan cheese
1 (8-ounce) package cream cheese, softened
1/4 cup sour cream
2 cloves garlic, minced
1 tablespoon minced fresh parsley
2 tablespoons minced fresh thyme
3 tablespoons fresh lemon juice

■ Preheat oven to 350°.
■ Remove stems from mushrooms. Wipe caps clean with a damp paper towel.
■ Brush mushrooms with melted butter and place in a 9 x 13 baking dish.
■ Combine remaining ingredients until well blended. Pipe evenly into the mushroom caps. Bake for 20 to 25 minutes.

Note: The recipe for Stuffed Mushrooms is designed specifically for petite-sized mushrooms, so check with your local grocer at least a week before your party to ensure availability.

S'more Brownies
Makes 2 dozen

1 family-size brownie mix, which yields a 9x13 pan of brownies
10 whole graham cracker squares, broken into pieces
2 cups miniature marshmallows
1 cup Hershey's milk chocolate chips

■ Preheat oven to 350°.
■ Lightly grease a 13x9x2-inch baking pan. Mix brownie mix according to package directions. Pour into prepared pan. Bake 18 minutes.
■ Remove from oven. Sprinkle with graham cracker pieces, pressing down lightly. Sprinkle evenly with marshmallows and chocolate chips. Return to oven, and continue baking 12 minutes. Let cool, and cut into 24 squares.

Creamy Lemon Petit Fours
Makes about 2 dozen

2 (16-ounce) prepared pound cakes
1 recipe Creamy Lemon Filling (recipe follows)
1 (1 1/2-pound) package vanilla or white chocolate candy coating
1/2 to 1 block paraffin
Sliced almonds
Candied lemon zest (see note below)

■ Trim outer crust from pound cake. Slice horizontally into 3 even layers. With a 2-inch square cutter or knife, slice pound cake into even squares.
■ Spread lemon filling between two layers of pound cake and sandwich together. Place on a cookie sheet and freeze for 1 hour.
■ Melt candy coating and paraffin in microwave or double boiler. With a skewer, dip each sandwich to coat. Place on baking rack with wax paper underneath. Allow to dry.
■ Garnish with a small dollop of white candy coating or almond bark, sliced almonds, and candied lemon zest.

Creamy Lemon Filling:
Makes 1 cup

5 egg yolks
3/4 cup sugar
1/3 cup fresh lemon juice
Zest of 3 lemons
1/2 cup heavy whipping cream
1/2 teaspoon vanilla extract
1/2 cup unsalted butter, cut into pieces

■ In top of double boiler, whisk together egg yolks, sugar, lemon juice, and zest until blended.
■ Over simmering water, cook mixture 7 to 8 minutes, whisking constantly, until thickened. Add cream, and cook 2 minutes.
■ Remove from heat; add vanilla. Whisk in butter, 1 tablespoon at a time.
■ Cover with plastic wrap, touching the surface of filling to prevent skin from forming. Can be stored up to 1 month in refrigerator.

Note: To candy lemon zest, mix 1/2 cup sugar and 1/2 cup water in a saucepan over high heat. Heat to a boil and add lemon zest. Cook for about 5 minutes, until translucent in appearance.

Creamy Lemon Petit Fours

Stuffed Mushrooms

S'more Brownies

ABOVE and LEFT: Artful hors d'ouvres and delicious desserts are stars in this bite-sized buffet. A platter full of Stuffed Mushrooms gets the party going while delightfully simple treats in the form of S'more Brownies and Creamy Lemon Petit Fours end the soiree in the sweetest way—bringing happy smiles and many thanks for a most enjoyable afternoon.

poolside grill
For the Bride & Groom

Fire up the grill and serve up good times aplenty. Waters so blue and plants so lush set the relaxed, almost exotic atmosphere that makes this extraordinary party one to remember for years to come.

Whether a rehearsal dinner or a shower of sorts, a poolside shindig provides the perfect setting to celebrate the beginning of two lives joining together as one. Bright and crisp colors create a Mediterranean-like ambiance that sweeps those in attendance away into an idyllic world of festivity.

Able to accommodate a large number of guests, plush seating areas offer an abundance of cushy spots to sit and chat. A choose-a-cocktail table starts the pre-wedding bash off with a particularly personal panache, a theme that repeats itself with a create-your-own grillable feast.

Two grill stations complete with expert chefs offer dinner options galore, giving hungry partygoers a chance to suit their culinary cravings. Dining and mingling continue, and as daylight fades into darkness, dozens upon dozens of candles illuminate the magical scene. The happy couple offers sincerest thanks and gratitude to those who have shown support over the years and now share in this special moment. Exchanging best wishes with toasting glasses, all in attendance bask in the reflections of hope and happiness glistening in the rippling waters of the pool, a picture of the friendship and fellowship that forever will be true blue.

So serene and inviting, the glow of more than 100 candles lights the way for the many guests to mingle and meander from the deck to the patio to the pool. With such an expansive area for merrymaking, the decorations and theme can prove to be challenging and costly, but with a little creativity, you can fill the space with enchanting accents without breaking the bank.

Gather lanterns, torches, and other illuminating items from your friends and neighbors, and fashion additional hanging lamps with inexpensive glass globes, tealight candles, and wire from the local hardware store. Floating candles in an array of glass hurricane containers can be filled with water and flowers to add to the aquatic ambiance, while pillar candles centered on floating hosta badges gently flicker like tiny water sprites in the pool. Durable and hefty Styrofoam provides the platform for these drifting décor items, and once carefully secured with florist wire and hot glue, your creations will lend themselves to the overall look of luminous loveliness.

From tiny tealights to towering pillars, countless candles shine as the central decorating elements for this extra-special event that celebrates a lasting union.

Aqua blues and apple greens provide a most becoming background for this island-inspired soiree designed to entertain a large number of guests.

By sticking to a basic color palette, you can bring the theme of your party to life in a variety of ways. Start with bright bamboo placemats in Granny Smith apple-green, followed by chic cerulean napkins folded into a clever pocket (see page 27 for step-by-step instructions). With these colors as the foundation of your design, add complementing accents, such as a beautiful bowlful of citrus fruits.

Subtle ivory and cream flowers pair with vivid blue and green decorative marbles to make eye-catching table displays that match the fabric and patterns of the surrounding patio furniture. These water-filled goblets also coordinate with the colors of the nearby swimming pool, creating a certain charisma and continuity that flows through the entire event.

For those who have devoted countless hours of help and offered continuous support over the years, "thank you" never seems to be enough. Nevertheless, that two-word phrase goes a long way in expressing gratitude, especially when it's combined with a small token of appreciation. Inside a patterned-paper packet, inscribe a few sentiments and place a pouch of special seasonings for guests to use the next time they fire up their own grills. Not only will this inspire perhaps another outdoor gathering, but it will also remind dear ones how much they truly mean to you.

Menu

Green Apple Spritzer

Watermelon Spritz

Bruschetta

Tapenade

Pistachio Grape Relish

Roma Vinaigrette Salsa

Gorgonzola and Pistachio Salad

Grilled Ratatouille

Grilled Quail

Grilled Tuna

Grilled Brie and Pears

Entertaining Touches

The trio of toppings, which includes Tapenade, Roma Vinaigrette Salsa, and Pistachio Grape Relish, is designed to work with this grilled feast in several ways. Whether guests select Bruschetta, Grilled Quail, or Grilled Tuna (see the following recipes for serving suggestions), they can choose their favorite flavors and create their own cuisine; the mixing and matching makes the dining more fun.

Tapenade
Pistachio Grape Relish
Roma Vinaigrette Salsa
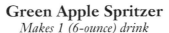

Bruschetta

Green Apple Spritzer
Makes 1 (6-ounce) drink

3 ounces sparkling mineral water
2 ounces Tuaca Italian Liqueur®
1 ounce Rose's® green apple drink infuser

■ Fill an 8-ounce glass with ice. Combine ingredients and pour over ice.

Watermelon Spritz
Makes 1 (6-ounce) drink

4 ounces sparkling mineral water
2 ounces Rose's® watermelon drink infuser

■ Fill an 8-ounce glass with ice. Combine ingredients and pour over ice.

Bruschetta
Makes 4 to 6 servings

1 (1-pound) French baguette
1/4 cup olive oil
1/4 teaspoon dried thyme leaves
1/4 teaspoon garlic powder
1/4 teaspoon rubbed sage

■ Split baguette in half lengthwise. In a small bowl, combine remaining ingredients. Brush olive oil mixture evenly on baguette halves.
■ Grill baguette, cut side down, 1 to 2 minutes, until golden brown.
■ Slice each half into 3-inch slices. Serve with Roma Vinaigrette Salsa or Tapenade.

Tapenade
Makes 12 to 14 servings

1 cup marinated olives, chopped
2 tablespoons chopped fresh parsley
1 clove garlic, minced
Zest and juice of 1 lemon

■ In a small bowl, combine all ingredients.

Pistachio Grape Relish
Makes 10 to 12 servings

20 white seedless grapes, chopped
15 red seedless grapes, chopped
³/₄ cup shelled pistachio nuts

■ Combine all ingredients in a medium bowl. Cover and chill until ready to serve.

Roma Vinaigrette Salsa
Makes 10 to 12 servings

3 Roma tomatoes, diced
3 fresh basil leaves, thinly sliced
2 cloves garlic, minced
¹/₄ cup chopped red onion
¹/₄ cup olive oil
¹/₄ cup chopped fresh parsley
3 tablespoons balsamic vinegar
1 teaspoon salt

■ Combine all ingredients in a medium bowl. Cover and let stand 15 minutes before serving.

RIGHT: Crumbled Gorgonzola cheese, dried cranberries, and pistachio nuts are the finishing touches that make this spring-mix salad so taste-tempting. Add the special dressing blend just before serving, or offer it on the side so guests can splash or dash on the amount they desire.

Gorgonzola and Pistachio Salad

Grilling Perfection

grilling perfection

When hosting a party of this size, you'll likely want to recruit several capable cooks from the family to help man the grilling stations, or you may want to simply hire a chef or two (we suggest one chef for every 10 guests). But if you are entertaining on a smaller scale and want to do the grilling yourself, here are a few tried-and-true tips to help ensure success.

- Set up the grill in the open air on level ground that's at least several feet away from the house or shelter.

- When first trying a recipe, follow the instructions closely to gauge what the end result will look and taste like, and then make adjustments accordingly to achieve optimum results for your personal tastes.

- Use the right utensils. Long-handled tools and barbecue mitts help protect you from the heat. Use tongs or turners to rotate foods. Only use forks to lift fully cooked foods in order to avoid piercing, which could result in loss of flavorful juices.

- As a general health rule, marinades should not be reused, but if you must, be sure to boil them first for a minimum of two minutes.

- Have clean platters and utensils on-hand for cooked foods; never put cooked foods back onto platters that were used for raw meats.

- When it comes to game such as quail, cooked muscle meats may be pink even when the meat has reached a safe internal temperature. If fresh game has reached 160°F throughout, even though it may still be pink in the center, it should be safe. When in doubt about doneness in regards to game or otherwise, use a thermometer to gauge internal temperatures. For more information, consult the U.S. Food and Drug Administration at *www.fda.gov*.

Grilled Ratatouille

Grilled Quail
Grilled Tuna

Gorgonzola and Pistachio Salad
Makes 4 servings

1 (5-ounce) package spring mix or mesclun mix
4 ounces Gorgonzola cheese, crumbled
³/₄ cup shelled pistachio nuts
¹/₂ cup dried cranberries
4 tablespoons balsamic vinegar
3 tablespoons hazelnut oil
3 tablespoons olive oil

■ In a medium bowl, combine spring mix, cheese, pistachio nuts, and cranberries.
■ In a small bowl, whisk together remaining ingredients. Pour dressing over salad, tossing gently to coat. Serve immediately.

Grilled Ratatouille
Makes 10 to 12 servings

1 sweet potato, peeled and cut into ¹/₄-inch slices
4 cloves garlic, chopped
3 Roma tomatoes, quartered
2 zucchini, cut in half lengthwise and crosswise
1 eggplant, cut into ¹/₂-inch slices
1 red onion, cut into 8 pieces
³/₄ cup olive oil
1 teaspoon fresh rosemary leaves
¹/₂ teaspoon salt
¹/₂ teaspoon freshly ground black pepper

■ Blanch sweet potato slices in boiling water 2 to 3 minutes; drain. In a large mixing bowl, combine all ingredients, tossing to coat vegetables.
■ Cook vegetables, without grill lid, over high heat (400° to 500°) 6 to 8 minutes, or until tender.

Grilled Quail
Makes 4 servings

4 whole quail
6 cloves garlic, chopped
1 sprig fresh rosemary
3 tablespoons hazelnut oil
1 tablespoon raspberry vinegar
1 tablespoon black fig vinegar
1 teaspoon salt
¹/₄ teaspoon lemon juice

■ Using kitchen sheers, cut down both sides of backbone and remove. Split each quail in half and remove rib bones. Remove first joint from each wing. Remove tip from each drumstick.
■ Combine quail and remaining ingredients in a resealable plastic bag; refrigerate 2 hours. Remove quail from marinade, discarding marinade.
■ Cook quail, without grill lid, over high heat (400° to 500°) 6 to 8 minutes, or until desired degree of doneness. Serve with Pistachio Grape Relish or Roma Vinaigrette Salsa.

Grilled Tuna
Makes 4 servings

4 fresh tuna steaks (about 1¹/₂ pounds total)
6 cloves garlic, chopped
2 sprigs fresh rosemary
3 tablespoons olive oil
1 tablespoon balsamic vinegar
Juice of 2 lemons (about 6 tablespoons)

■ Combine tuna and remaining ingredients in a resealable plastic bag; refrigerate 2 hours. Remove tuna from marinade, discarding marinade.
■ Cook tuna, without grill lid, over high heat (400° to 500°) 3 to 4 minutes, or until desired degree of doneness. Serve with Pistachio Grape Relish or Roma Vinaigrette Salsa.

Grilled Brie and Pears
Makes 12 to 15 servings

2 (4-ounce) Brie wheels
¹/₂ cup honey
1 cup sliced almonds
8 pears

■ Coat Brie with honey. Place Brie on grill and sear. Turn over and top with sliced almonds. Close grill lid and cook until cheese is plump, 1 to 2 minutes.
■ Slice pears in half lengthwise. Place on grill and cook 1 minute.
■ To serve, place Brie on serving platter; garnish with grilled pears.

Grilled Brie and Pears

Royal Rewards

According to legend, eighth-century French Emperor Charlemagne first tasted Brie in a monastery in Reuil-en-Brie and immediately fell in love with this soft cheese's creamy, rich flavor. Brie, which once graced only the tables of royalty, eventually reached the masses, securing its widespread popularity. True French Brie, made in an area south of Paris, cannot be imported to the States, but many countries now make a similar cheese that is sold as Brie. This version of the long-time favorite is often served with vegetables and meat, but it is best known as an elegant and decadent part of dessert due to its fruity flavor and gooey center.

on the lawn
Golden Afternoon

An old-fashioned pursuit replete with fine linens, family silver, and filling refreshments, this lawn party brings friends together for fun, frivolity, and a spirited game of croquet.

Mallets in hand, women clothed in white linen join men in slacks and shirts of the same color as they all make their way through a carefully arranged course. Good-natured taunting and witty interludes are interrupted only when, in turn, each in the merry party pauses to send a wooden ball rolling across the well-manicured lawn through a nearby wicket. The camaraderie is strong, the competition lively.

This scene could depict one from 1850s England, the Roaring Twenties in America, or a 21st-century backyard, for croquet has long been favored as a particularly delightful way to spend an afternoon. No one quite knows just where or how the game originated, but regardless of whether Italy, France, or Egypt actually holds bragging rights, the sequenced sport with hoops and balls continues to draw a crowd.

Appropriate for the young, old, and in-between, croquet provides a magnificent mix of etiquette and exercise. It also offers a variety of course possibilities, allowing players to choose the level of difficulty. Best of all, those in attendance get the chance to spend a lovely afternoon outdoors, enjoying the pleasures of splendid company.

The Fashions of Croquet

It is a long-standing and always respected tradition to wear white clothing while playing the very genteel game of croquet. The image of players in pristine linen—long dresses for the ladies and "Gatsby" knickers for the gents—is impossible to separate from the mallets and wickets of the game itself. In homage to this tradition, we continue to attire ourselves in white from head to toe when we step onto the grass playing field for an afternoon of friendly croquet competition. Women may wear skirts, pants, or culottes paired with blouses and sweaters, depending on what the weather dictates; for men, either trousers or shorts are acceptable. All participants should wear flat-soled shoes so as not to mar the course. Jaunty straw hats are not required, but they surely add to the fun.

Croquetiquette

To ensure a pleasant outing, here are a few suggestions for proper etiquette on the croquet lawn:

- There are many variations of the game. Determine the course to be played and the rules beforehand.

- Respect your fellow players by remaining quiet during play.

- Move out of another player's line of sight when he or she addresses the ball.

- Play in a timely fashion, maintaining the flow of the game.

- Honor the tradition of the game by being well mannered and attentive during play.

Menu

Strawberry Bellini

Sunshine Punch

Individual Fruit Trifles

Tomato, Basil, and Mozzarella Salad

Endive Boats with Fresh Fruit Salad

Shredded Pork Croissants with Spicy Peach Chutney

In keeping with the easy, breezy feel of a relaxing afternoon, plan a menu that is simple to prepare. Seasonal fruits effortlessly add splashes of color and bursts of juicy delights to the spread. With the sun high in the azure sky, temperatures will warm, increasing the need for refreshing beverages, so be sure to have an ample selection available. Salads and savory sandwiches are the order of the day. Include dishes that can be prepared ahead of time, leaving you free to mingle with guests and play the course a time or two.

Strawberry Bellini

Sunshine Punch

ABOVE: Whether you choose to make this beverage with champagne or ginger ale, a Strawberry Bellini offers delightful refreshment on a sunny afternoon. A fresh strawberry, used as a garnish, adds a tempting touch.

ABOVE: A blend of fruit juices mixed with fizzy ginger ale makes Sunshine Punch the perfect thirst quencher. Add a sliver of the sun—an orange slice—to float lazily on top.

OPPOSITE: Luscious layers of summertime fruits are tiered with fluffy whipped cream and a base of golden pound cake. Fresh fruit slices top off this light-and-lively dessert, enticing guests to put down their croquet mallets and pick up their forks.

Strawberry Bellini
Makes 6 servings

1 (10-ounce) package frozen halved strawberries in syrup, thawed
2 tablespoons strawberry liqueur (optional)
1 bottle (750-ml) chilled champagne or 1 (2-liter) bottle ginger ale

In a blender, puree strawberries and strawberry liqueur. In a fluted glass, spoon 1 tablespoon strawberry puree and add chilled champagne or ginger ale. Stir gently and serve. Refrigerate and reserve remaining strawberry puree for another use.

Sunshine Punch
Makes 3 quarts

3 cups orange juice
3 cups apple juice
3 cups pineapple juice
3 cups chilled ginger ale

In a large container, combine orange juice, apple juice, and pineapple juice. Refrigerate overnight to allow flavors to blend. Just prior to serving, add ginger ale.

Individual Fruit Trifles
Makes 4 to 6 servings

1 (3.3-ounce) package white chocolate instant pudding
1 cup milk
1 cup heavy whipping cream
1/2 cup sour cream
1 1/2 cups sliced fresh strawberries
1 1/2 cups chopped kiwi
1 1/2 cups fresh blueberries
Prepared or commercial pound cake

■ In a large mixing bowl, combine pudding mix and milk. Beat with an electric mixer at medium speed until smooth. Add cream and sour cream, beating until soft peaks form.
■ To assemble, cut pound cake to fit dish. Layer cake, pudding mixture, and fruit. Repeat layers as desired. Refrigerate until ready to serve.

Individual Fruit Trifles

Tomato, Basil, and Mozzarella Salad

Tomato, Basil, and Mozzarella Salad
Makes 4 to 6 servings

2 medium red tomatoes, sliced to ¼-inch
  thickness
2 medium yellow tomatoes, sliced to ¼-inch
  thickness
2 (8-ounce) packages fresh Mozzarella, sliced to
  ¼-inch thickness
¼ cup finely shredded fresh basil
1 recipe Balsamic Vinaigrette (recipe follows)

■ Layer tomato slices, cheese, and basil. Top
with Balsamic Vinaigrette.

Balsamic Vinaigrette:
Makes ⅔ cup

¼ cup balsamic vinegar
1 teaspoon sugar
¼ teaspoon salt
¼ teaspoon ground black pepper
½ cup olive oil

■ In a medium bowl, combine vinegar, sugar,
salt, and pepper. Whisk until sugar dissolves.
Whisking constantly, gradually add olive oil
until well combined.

Endive Boats with Fresh Fruit Salad
Makes 6 servings

½ cup fresh orange juice
1 tablespoon confectioners' sugar
1 tablespoon honey
½ cup halved seedless red grapes
½ cup chopped banana
½ cup fresh orange sections
½ cup chopped red apple
½ cup chopped green apple
6 Belgian endive lettuce leaves

■ In a small bowl, combine orange juice, sugar,
and honey; set aside.
■ In a medium bowl, combine grapes, bananas,
oranges, and apples. Pour orange juice mixture
over fruit and gently toss.
■ Cover and chill for 2 hours or more. Serve
in endive leaves.

Shredded Pork Croissants with Spicy Peach Chutney
Makes 4 to 6 servings

1 (2-pound) boneless pork loin, trimmed
½ teaspoon salt
½ teaspoon ground black pepper
¼ cup olive oil
3 cloves garlic, minced
2 cups chicken broth
4 to 6 croissants
1 head leaf lettuce, finely shredded
1 recipe Spicy Peach Chutney (recipe follows)

■ Cut pork loin in half length-wise; season with
salt and pepper. In a Dutch oven, heat olive oil
over medium-high heat. Add pork loin, brown-
ing all sides. Remove pork loin and sauté garlic
for 1 to 2 minutes. Return pork loin to pan,
reduce heat to medium-low and add chicken
broth. Cover and simmer for 1½ to 2 hours,
until tender, turning meat every 30 minutes.
Remove from heat and cool 10 minutes. With
two forks, shred meat into bite-size pieces.
■ To assemble sandwiches, slice croissants in half
horizontally. On bottom half of each croissant, layer
lettuce and pork; top with Spicy Peach Chutney.

Spicy Peach Chutney:
Makes 2 cups

1 tablespoon butter
1 tablespoon garlic, minced
1 jalapeño pepper, seeded and minced
2 medium shallots, minced
3 cups chopped fresh peaches
½ cup golden raisins
¼ cup sugar
1 tablespoon apple cider vinegar
1 tablespoon lemon juice
1 teaspoon salt
1 teaspoon hot sauce
½ teaspoon black pepper

■ In a large saucepan, melt butter over medium heat. Add garlic, jalapeño, and shallot;
cook for 2 to 3 minutes. Add peaches and
raisins; cook for 2 to 3 minutes. Stir in sugar,
mixing well. Stir in vinegar, lemon juice, salt,
hot sauce, and pepper. Simmer for 5 to 10
minutes on low heat until peaches and raisins
become soft. Serve warm.

Endive Boats with Fresh Fruit Salad

Shredded Pork Croissants with Spicy Peach Chutney

ABOVE: Five fresh fruits combine in a dainty
lettuce boat for a salad as bright as a sunshiny
day. Treat guests to tender pork loin slices piled
high on flaky croissants—available for purchase
at your local bakery—and topped with Spicy
Peach Chutney.

OPPOSITE: Eye-catching bands of color in the
Tomato, Basil, and Mozzarella Salad make
this dish irresistible. Slice the layers as evenly
as possible, especially the base layer, so that
when drizzled with Balsamic Vinaigrette, you'll
have a sturdy, stand-up presentation.

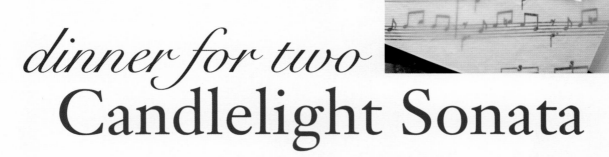

dinner for two
Candlelight Sonata

The evening sky still blushes from the sun's pink and golden descent. Flickering like fireflies, candles light the way through a private garden to a table set for two. Soft music fills the air. Romance is all around.

Soft but clear, the melody from the strings of a single violin permeates the lush surroundings, whispering enchantment in every note. Another instrument joins in with harmony so bewitching that even the leaves in the trees seem to sway in one accord. In a cozy courtyard, you and your beloved each take a seat at a most inviting table.

Dripping candles in an exquisite, antique candelabra cast their rosy glow across this captivating scene, and gold-rimmed glass plates echo the illumination with a faint reflection. Five artful and flavorful courses grace the table—Roasted Walnut Salad, Seared Scallops, Four Flower Sorbet, and more—indulging the senses in every possible way.

After drinking and dining into a state of utter contentment, the music once again begins its magical strains, calling to the heart with each beat, each measure, each refrain. A slow dance in the arms of the one you love counts each step as an affirmation of the bond and devotion you share, and hand in hand with your sweetheart, you drift away in the music of this very special evening.

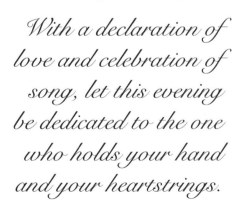

With a declaration of love and celebration of song, let this evening be dedicated to the one who holds your hand and your heartstrings.

Thoughtful details and meaningful additions help turn an ordinary meal outdoors into an extraordinary escape for you and the one you love. A lovely handwritten note, strategically placed for an element of surprise, invites your beloved to come away with you for a night of unexpected delights.

Set the table in an area that ensures privacy, and press the linens ahead of time to save precious moments on the day of the dinner. When creating an arrangement for the table, consider incorporating a mixture of posies and vegetables to infuse the setting with lush color, and seek floral varieties that symbolize something special, such as the hues of your wedding. Complete the ambiance by assembling a series of significant songs that speak of times the two of you have shared, and coordinate a stringed quartet or even a single violinist to play these memorable melodies throughout the evening.

Menu

*Roasted Walnut Salad with
Creamy Mint Dressing*

Seared Scallops

Four Flower Sorbet

*Pan-Roasted Duck Breast with
Asparagus and Corn Relish*

*Red Anjou Pears with
Blueberry Wine and Homemade
Vanilla Ice Cream*

Roasted Walnut Salad with Creamy Mint Dressing

Entertaining Touches

Since the focus of this occasion is spending time with your sweetheart, it's important to allow plenty of prep time so that you, too, can enjoy the evening. You may even want to recruit the assistance of a chef to prepare this exquisite menu, leaving you more time for pressing and dressing.

Roasted Walnut Salad with Creamy Mint Dressing
Makes 2 servings

2 baby golden beets
3 tablespoons water
$1/3$ cup walnuts
1 teaspoon olive oil
2 cups heavy whipping cream
2 tablespoons champagne vinegar
$1/2$ cup fresh mint leaves, chopped
2 small heads Boston or Bibb lettuce, washed and dried
Salt, to taste
Freshly ground black pepper, to taste
Garnish: fresh mint leaves, cut into thin strips

■ Preheat oven to 375°. Place beets in an 8x8x2-inch pan. Pour water in bottom of pan, and cover tightly with aluminum foil. Bake 10 to 15 minutes, or until beets are tender; uncover and cool completely. Peel beets and cut into quarters; set aside.
■ In a small bowl, combine walnuts and oil; season to taste with salt, stirring to coat nuts evenly. Place on a baking sheet, and bake at 375° for 5 to 7 minutes, or until golden brown; cool.
■ In a small bowl, whisk together cream and vinegar until mixture thickens slightly. Add mint, stirring to mix well. Season to taste with salt and pepper. Cover and refrigerate until ready to use.
■ To serve, place lettuce in a medium bowl. Gradually add enough dressing to coat leaves, tossing gently. Top with beets and walnuts. Garnish with fresh mint, if desired.

Seared Scallops
Makes 2 servings

2 tablespoons olive oil
4 large fresh sea scallops
Salt, to taste
Freshly ground black pepper, to taste
1 recipe Ragout of Spring Vegetables (recipe follows)
1 recipe Lemon Butter Sauce (recipe follows)
Garnish: flat-leaf parsley

■ In a large non-stick skillet, heat oil over medium-high heat. Add scallops; cook for 2 to 3 minutes on each side, until golden brown. Season to taste with salt and pepper.
■ To serve, spoon Ragout of Spring Vegetables on plate; top with 2 scallops and Lemon Butter Sauce. Garnish with parsley, if desired.

Ragout of Spring Vegetables:
Makes 2 servings

2 baby candy-striped beets or baby red beets
3 tablespoons water
1 tablespoon olive oil
6 baby carrots, parboiled and quartered
2 small purple Peruvian potatoes, parboiled and quartered
6 sugar snap peas, blanched and shocked
Salt, to taste
Freshly ground black pepper, to taste

■ Preheat oven to 375°. Place beets in an 8x8x2-inch pan. Pour water in bottom of pan, and cover tightly with aluminum foil. Bake 10 to 15 minutes, or until beets are tender; uncover and cool completely. Peel beets and cut into quarters; set aside.
■ In a medium skillet, heat 1 tablespoon olive oil over medium heat. Add beets, carrots, potatoes,

recipe continues to next page...

Seared Scallops

Pan-Roasted Duck Breast with Asparagus and Corn Relish

and peas; sauté 3 to 4 minutes. Season to taste with salt and pepper.

Lemon Butter Sauce:
Makes 2 to 4 servings

1 shallot, minced
2 sprigs fresh thyme
1 bay leaf
1/2 cup white wine
1/3 cup white-wine vinegar
1 tablespoon heavy whipping cream
1 pound unsalted butter, cut into cubes
Juice of 2 lemons (about 6 tablespoons)
Salt, to taste
Freshly ground black pepper, to taste

■ In a medium saucepan, combine shallot, thyme, bay leaf, white wine, and vinegar over high heat. Bring to a boil and cook 5 to 6 minutes, or until 3 tablespoons of liquid remains.
■ Remove from heat; add cream; reduce heat to low and slowly whisk in butter. Stir in lemon juice; season with salt and pepper. Strain sauce through a fine-mesh strainer, discarding solids; serve warm.

Four Flower Sorbet
Makes 12 to 15 servings

3 cups sugar
3 cups water
3 tablespoons corn syrup
2 cups fresh orange juice
3/4 cup fresh lemon juice
2 tablespoons grenadine syrup
1 vanilla bean, split lengthwise
1 recipe Blood Orange Chips (recipe follows)

■ In a medium saucepan, combine sugar, water, and corn syrup over medium heat. Cook 10 minutes, stirring frequently, until sugar is completely dissolved; cool completely.
■ In a large bowl, combine orange juice, lemon juice, grenadine, and vanilla bean. Add sugar syrup, stirring to combine well. Strain through a fine-mesh strainer, discarding solids.
■ Place mixture in ice cream freezer and freeze according to manufacturer's instructions, until firm; store in freezer.
■ To serve, pipe sorbet into dish and garnish with Blood Orange Chips.

Blood Orange Chips:
Makes about 20 pieces

2 medium blood oranges
3 (12-ounce) bottles grenadine syrup

■ Preheat oven to 100°. Line a baking sheet with parchment paper; set aside. Wash oranges and dry thoroughly. Cut thin slices of orange. Combine orange slices and grenadine in a heavy-duty resealable plastic bag.
■ Fill a Dutch oven halfway with water; bring to a boil over high heat. Place sealed plastic bag in water and return to a boil. Reduce heat to low; simmer 10 minutes.
■ Carefully remove bag from water; drain orange slices through a strainer. Lay orange slices flat on prepared baking sheet.
■ Bake 8 to 10 hours, or until completely dry. Store in airtight container until needed.

Pan-Roasted Duck Breast with Asparagus and Corn Relish
Makes 2 servings

2 stalks green asparagus
2 stalks white asparagus
1 tablespoon extra virgin olive oil, divided
2 ears red or yellow corn, cut off cob
1 teaspoon champagne vinegar
1 teaspoon chopped fresh chives
2 Hudson Valley duck breasts
Salt, to taste
Freshly ground black pepper, to taste
1 recipe Creamy Polenta (recipe follows)
1 recipe Sauce Beurre Rouge (recipe follows)

■ Trim asparagus 1 1/2 inches below the tip; cook in boiling, salted water 1 minute. Cool in ice water, and dry; set aside.
■ In a small skillet, heat 1 1/2 teaspoons oil over medium-high heat. Sauté corn 3 to 4 minutes, or until tender; cool.
■ In a small bowl, combine asparagus, corn, 1 1/2 teaspoons oil, vinegar, and chives. Season to taste with salt and pepper. Stir to combine; set aside.
■ Pat duck breasts dry with a paper towel. With a sharp knife, score skin on duck breasts. Season both sides of duck breasts with salt and pepper.

Artful Presentations

Presenting your delicious dishes creatively can elevate them to magnum opus status. If the recipe calls for a sauce, borrow inspiration from professional chefs and swirl it around—instead of on top of—the main food item. Consider colors and textures before assembling the final plated dish, and if it's a particularly special occasion, practice beforehand to perfect the food's placement and position. Use your imagination to present culinary concoctions in unconventional ways, such as the skillfully chiseled ice sculpture basket bearing a cold and refreshing sorbet shown on the opposite page.

- Preheat oven to 375°. In a cast iron skillet, place duck breasts, skin side down, over medium-high heat. Cook 5 to 8 minutes, until skin browns. Place skillet in oven and cook to an internal temperature of 165°, or desired degree of doneness.
- To serve, spoon polenta on center of plate. Thinly slice duck breast, and place around polenta, skin side up. Spoon asparagus relish over top. Top with Sauce Beurre Rouge.

Creamy Polenta:
Makes 2 to 4 servings

1 cup heavy whipping cream
1 cup chicken broth
1 cup polenta
1 tablespoon butter
1 tablespoon freshly grated Parmesan cheese
Salt, to taste
Freshly ground black pepper, to taste

- In a medium saucepan over high heat, combine cream and chicken broth; bring to a boil. Gradually add polenta, stirring constantly. Reduce heat to low, and cook 20 minutes, stirring frequently.
- Stir in butter and Parmesan cheese; season to taste with salt and pepper. Serve warm.

Sauce Beurre Rouge:
Makes 2 to 4 servings

2 shallots, minced
2 sprigs fresh thyme
1 bay leaf
1/2 cup red wine
1/3 cup red-wine vinegar
1 tablespoon heavy whipping cream
1 pound butter, cut into cubes
Juice of 1 lemon (about 3 tablespoons)
Salt, to taste

- In a small sauce pan over high heat, combine shallots, thyme, bay leaf, wine, and vinegar. Bring to a boil and cook 5 to 6 minutes, or until 3 tablespoons of liquid remains. Remove from heat, and add cream; reduce heat to low and slowly whisk in butter.
- Stir in lemon juice, and season to taste with salt. Strain sauce through a fine-mesh strainer; serve warm.

Four Flower Sorbet

Red Anjou Pears with Blueberry Wine and Homemade Vanilla Ice Cream

Makes 4 servings

2 cups sugar
2 cups water
1 (750-ml) bottle Morgan Creek® blueberry wine
2 cinnamon sticks
4 bay leaves
8 black peppercorns, crushed
1 strip orange peel
4 Red Anjou pears
1 pint fresh blueberries
1 large egg
1 cup flour
1 cup ice-cold water
Vegetable oil for frying
4 sprigs fresh lemon thyme
2 ladyfingers
1 recipe Homemade Vanilla Ice Cream (recipe follows)

■ In a medium saucepan, combine sugar and water over medium heat. Cook 10 minutes, stirring frequently, until sugar is completely dissolved; cool completely.

■ Line a baking sheet with parchment paper; set aside. In a Dutch oven, combine wine, cinnamon sticks, bay leaves, peppercorns, orange peel, and sugar syrup over medium-high heat.

■ Peel pears and carefully hollow out center from the bottom, leaving stem end intact. Place pears in blueberry wine mixture and cover with lid. Bring to a boil, reduce heat and simmer 10 to 15 minutes. Remove pears from wine mixture and place on prepared baking sheet; refrigerate.

■ Strain wine mixture through a fine-mesh strainer, discarding solids, and pour back into Dutch oven. Bring to a boil over medium-high heat and cook until mixture thickens to a syrup consistency. Reduce heat to low and add blueberries. Remove from heat and set aside; keep warm.

■ In a small bowl, combine egg, flour, and water; whisk until smooth. In a small skillet, pour oil to a 1/2-inch depth. Heat oil to 350° over medium heat. Dip lemon thyme in egg mixture and fry 1 minute per side, or until lightly browned. Drain on paper towels; set aside.

■ Cut ladyfingers to fit bottom of pear. Preheat broiler. Line a baking sheet with parchment paper; set aside.

■ To serve, pipe ice cream into center of each pear, leaving a 1/4-inch space at base. Seal ice cream into pears with ladyfinger pieces. Immediately broil 5 1/2 inches from heat (with door of oven partially opened) for 1 to 2 minutes, or just until pear is warm.

■ Place each pear on plate and pour blueberry wine mixture over top. Garnish with prepared lemon thyme. Serve immediately.

Homemade Vanilla Ice Cream:

Makes 12 servings

8 egg yolks
2/3 cup sugar
1 tablespoon vanilla extract
2 cups milk
1 1/2 tablespoons corn syrup
1 vanilla bean, split
2/3 cup heavy whipping cream

■ In a medium bowl, whisk together egg yolks, sugar, and vanilla; set aside. In a medium saucepan, combine milk, corn syrup, and vanilla bean; carefully bring to a boil over medium heat.

■ Whisking constantly, very slowly pour milk mixture into egg mixture, until well combined. Pour mixture into a large saucepan over low heat. Cook 5 to 10 minutes, or until mixture thickens slightly; do not allow mixture to boil.

■ Pour through a fine-mesh strainer, discarding solids; stir in cream. Place mixture in ice cream freezer and freeze according to manufacturer's instructions, until firm; store in freezer.

Red Anjou Pears with Blueberry Wine and Homemade Vanilla Ice Cream

OPPOSITE: Though the Red Anjou Pears with Blueberry Wine and Homemade Vanilla Ice Cream must be served immediately after broiling, the ice cream can be made a day or two before to save time. Also be sure to try the blueberry wine mixture with various other desserts and dishes—it may soon become one of your favorite toppings.

Surprise Inside

On an evening filled with delights, the meal requires a dessert that is extraordinary. The secret of these Red Anjou pears is found inside in the form of unbelievably delicious vanilla ice cream. The frozen ice cream is piped into the center of each pear, secured with ladyfingers, and then briefly broiled to achieve an incredible meld of sensations. Served with a splendid mixture of spices and specialty blueberry wine from Alabama, this sweet treat artfully combines Southern flavors in a way that is nothing short of divine.

of faith & love
White Bible Ceremony

For generations, a simple ceremony involving the presentation of flowers by near and dear ones has helped pave the way for those who choose to travel the road of life together, joined by the bonds of holy matrimony.

An old Southern tradition, the White Bible Ceremony relies on the language of flowers to express the pillars of marriage. This custom, which usually takes place in the month before the wedding, emphasizes the importance of faith and love through the presentation of beautiful blossoms to the bride- and groom-to-be.

Reserved for close friends and relatives, the ceremony—followed by a reception—begins with the lighting of candles to symbolize God's presence. One by one, loved ones present the couple with different flowers, each stem representing principles on which to base their lives together.

Sincerity, love, purity, unity, passion, and Christian growth—these foundations in the form of yellow, red, white, and green florals build a lovely bouquet. The betrothed are then presented a satin ribbon that binds the flowers together, signifying the bonds shared by a husband and wife.

Finally, the host and hostess present the pair with a white Bible. Though its pages may be edged in gold and its cover made of fine leather, it's what's inside that matters most of all—the cornerstone of Christian marriage: The Word of God.

Take-home treasures of small ribbon-wrapped Bibles and beautifully boxed heirloom handkerchiefs remind guests of life's most precious gifts— faith and family.

White Bible Ceremony

The White Bible Ceremony is a presentation of two gifts: stems of symbolic flowers and the Word of God. As cherished family and friends step forward, a reader explains the significance of each offering.

ONE RED ROSE

Red roses are the traditional expression of love. As we place this red rose in your bouquet, remember that although your love for one another is the romantic kind, a Christian couple should also reflect Christian love for others.

ONE YELLOW ROSE

A yellow rose represents sincerity. As we place this yellow rose in your bouquet, remember that a husband and wife should radiate sincere love and commitment toward each other. According to Philippians 2:3-4, the most successful marriages are those where both people respect and care for one another.

ONE RED AND ONE WHITE ROSE

The red and white roses represent unity. As we place these roses in your bouquet, think of Isaac and Rebekah. Each loved the other as the Psalmist said we should love God, with "all that is within me," body, mind, and soul. Because each was united within, they were happily united to each other.

ONE RED CARNATION

The red carnation signifies engagement and passion. You have made many decisions since you became engaged, and there will be many more for you to make. We pray that this carnation will remind you to always turn to God for guidance and leadership.

ONE WHITE CARNATION

The white carnation represents purity. God's word tells us that everyone who has hope in Christ keeps himself pure just as Christ is pure. We pray that your heart and home will be uncluttered with false standards and selfish ambitions.

GREENERY

In this bouquet, green foliage represents Christian growth. As we place this greenery in your bouquet, we pray that you may continue to grow in grace and in the knowledge of our Lord, inspiring others to grow in their faith as well.

RIBBON

The ribbon we give you now is to bind your bouquet together, just as your love should bind you. In your marriage vows, you will promise to take each other for better or worse, and we pray that in both good times and bad, the bonds of love will hold you together.

WHITE BIBLE

Let the white Bible be symbolic of a mutual love for God in your Christian home. We hope that you will turn to this book regularly for guidance, comfort, and assurance as you face the future together.

Cranberry Punch

Grilled Proscuitto Wrapped Asparagus
Gruyère Cream Puffs with Shrimp and Artichoke Filling

Cranberry Punch
Makes about 7 cups

4 cups cranberry juice, chilled
3 cups ginger ale, chilled
Garnish: fresh orange slices, fresh pineapple slices

■ In a large pitcher, combine cranberry juice and ginger ale. Garnish with fresh fruit, if desired.

Grilled Proscuitto-Wrapped Asparagus
Makes 40

¹/₂ pound Proscuitto very thinly sliced (40 slices)
40 asparagus stalks (about 1¹/₂ bunches)
2 tablespoons olive oil
Juice of 1 lemon

■ Wrap proscuitto around asparagus spears. Drizzle with olive oil and lemon juice. Grill over medium-high heat or bake at 450° until procuitto is crispy and lightly browned.

Gruyère Cream Puffs with Shrimp and Artichoke Filling
Makes 50

1 cup water
¹/₂ cup butter
¹/₈ teaspoon salt
1 cup all-purpose flour
4 large eggs
³/₄ cup shredded Gruyère cheese
¹/₄ cup butter
2 shallots, diced
1 pound medium fresh shrimp, peeled, de-veined, and chopped
1 (8-ounce) package cream cheese, softened
2 tablespoons half-and-half
1 (14-ounce) can artichoke hearts, drained and chopped
¹/₂ cup shredded Parmesan cheese
1 tablespoon chopped fresh parsley
1 tablespoon dry sherry
¹/₂ teaspoon salt

■ Preheat oven to 375°. In a medium saucepan, combine water, butter, and salt. Bring to a boil over medium-high heat. Add flour, and stir vigorously with a wooden spoon until mixture forms a ball. Let cool 3 minutes.
■ Using an electric mixer, beat in eggs, one at a time. Add Gruyère cheese, mixing well.
■ Spoon or pipe dough into 1-inch rounds onto parchment-lined baking sheets. Bake 22 to 25 minutes, or until puffed and golden. Let cool.
■ In a large saucepan, melt butter over medium heat. Add shallot and shrimp, and cook 3 to 4 minutes or until shrimp are firm. Stir in cream cheese, half-and-half, artichokes, Parmesan, parsley, sherry, and salt. Cook until cheeses are melted and mixture is combined.
■ Spoon filling evenly into prepared cream puffs, replacing cream puff top. Serve immediately.

Entertaining Touches

Although the White Bible Ceremony is formal in nature, the reception that follows can be casually elegant. Highlight a buffet brimming with goodies by strategically placing a few large arrangements that echo the soft white theme of the ceremony. Use recipes that can be made ahead of time, and prepare several trays full of dining delights that can wait in the wings until the spread is in need of replenishing.

Phyllo Napoleans with Kahlua Cream and Strawberries

────── *Doughs and Don'ts* ──────

Though phyllo dough has developed

a reputation for being difficult

to work with, a few tips can help

steer you to quite pleasing pastry

creations. Bear in mind that phyllo

dries out quickly once opened. Keep

it covered with a piece of wax paper

or a cool wet towel while you prepare

other ingredients. When brushing

with butter, don't saturate the dough.

A light coating is enough to prevent

wilting. Lastly, there's no use crying

over torn phyllo. If sheets buckle

or rip, you can "glue" them back

together with melted butter.

Mini Bittersweet Chocolate Cheesecakes with Hazelnut Chocolate Crust
Makes 4 dozen

2 cups crushed chocolate graham crackers
1 cup finely chopped toasted hazelnuts
1/2 cup sugar
3/4 cup plus 2 tablespoons butter, melted
4 (8-ounce) packages cream cheese, softened
1 cup sugar
2 large eggs plus 2 egg yolks
8 ounces bittersweet chocolate, melted
1/2 cup sour cream
1 teaspoon vanilla extract
Garnish: fresh blackberries, fresh raspberries

■ Preheat oven to 350°.
■ Combine crushed crackers, hazelnuts, sugar, and butter. Press mixture into bottoms of 4 (12-cup) mini cheesecake pans. Bake 8 minutes; cool completely.
■ In a large bowl, combine cream cheese and sugar. Beat with an electric mixer until creamy. Add eggs and egg yolks, one at a time, beating well after each addition. Stir in melted chocolate, sour cream, and vanilla.
■ Spoon mixture evenly into prepared pans. Bake 20 minutes. Cool completely. Chill 4 hours before removing from pans. Garnish with fresh berries, if desired.

Phyllo Napoleons with Kahlua Cream and Strawberries
Makes 4 dozen

1 envelope unflavored gelatin
1/4 cup cold water
1/3 cup boiling water
2 cups heavy whipping cream
1/2 cup sugar
5 tablespoons Kahlua® liqueur
1/2 (16-ounce) box frozen phyllo pastry sheets, thawed
1/2 cup butter, melted
1 (1-pound) package chocolate-flavored candy coating, melted
Garnish: fresh blackberries, fresh raspberries, confectioners' sugar

■ Soften gelatin in 1/4-cup cold water; let stand 2 minutes. Add boiling water, stirring until dis-solved; set aside.
■ In a large bowl, beat cream until thickened. Gradually add sugar, beating until stiff peaks form. Stir in Kahlua and gelatin mixture. (Mixture will look like it is melting but will firm up when chilled). Cover, and refrigerate 4 hours to overnight.
■ Preheat oven to 375°.
■ On a rimmed baking sheet, place 1 sheet phyllo. Brush with melted butter, and top with another phyllo sheet; brush with melted butter. Repeat procedure, forming 6 layers.
■ Cut phyllo layers into 2-inch squares. Bake 6 to 7 minutes, or until lightly browned. Remove to wire rack to cool completely. Dip 1 corner of half of phyllo squares in chocolate coating. Place on parchment paper to dry.
■ Place one un-dipped phyllo square on serving platter. Pipe Kahlua cream onto square; top with chocolate-dipped square. Repeat process. Garnish with fresh berries and confectioners' sugar, if desired.

Chilled Tenderloin Crostini with Gorgonzola Cream
Makes 40

40 thin baguette slices
1/4 cup olive oil, divided
1 (3-pound) beef tenderloin, trimmed
1/4 cup crushed peppercorns
1 recipe Balsamic Reduction (recipe follows)
1 recipe Gorgonzola Cream (recipe follows)
Garnish: fresh flat-leaf parsley

■ Preheat oven to 400°.
■ Brush baguette slices evenly with 2 table-spoons olive oil. Place on a baking sheet, and cook 10 to 12 minutes or until lightly toasted.
■ Preheat oven to 450°. Rub tenderloin with remaining olive oil. Roll tenderloin in crushed peppercorns. Place on rack in roasting pan and roast for 20 minutes.
■ Reduce heat to 350°. Cook for 20 to 25 minutes, or until a meat thermometer inserted into center reaches 145° (medium), or desired degree of doneness. Cool 30 minutes; cover and refrigerate 4 hours, or up to 1 day ahead.
■ To serve, slice tenderloin into 40 thin slices.

Chilled Tenderloin Crostini with Gorgonzola Cream

Place 1 slice tenderloin onto each crostini. Top with Gorgonzola Cream and Balsamic Reduction. Garnish with fresh parsley, if desired.

Balsamic Reduction:
Makes about ¼ cup

½ cup balsamic vinegar

■ In a small saucepan over medium-high heat, bring vinegar to a boil. Cook 5 to 6 minutes. Remove from heat and cool completely.

Gorgonzola Cream:
Makes 3 cups

1 pound Gorgonzola cheese
2 (8-ounce) packages cream cheese, softened
½ cup heavy whipping cream

■ Combine Gorgonzola and cream cheese in container of a food processor. Process until smooth.
■ In a medium bowl, beat cream until stiff peaks form. Fold whipped cream into cheese mixture. Chill.

ABOVE: Bite-sized yummies like crostinis leave guests free to weave in and out of rooms, plates in hand, bestowing greetings and warm wishes on the nearly newlyweds.

Mini Bittersweet Chocolate Cheesecakes with Hazelnut Chocolate Crust

gathered together
Home for the Holidays

Stockings are hung with the greatest of care above a happily crackling fire. White twinkle lights highlight handmade ornaments tucked into branches of a grandiose evergreen. Hands join hands in thanks for the many gifts of Christmas.

From near and far, family members have made the journey home to join together in the joys of Christmas. They bring not only presents but also glad hearts and good tidings. Hugs and handshakes galore greet them upon their arrival, and soon, everyone settles into the living room, basking in the brilliance of a dazzlingly decorated fir tree and comfortably familiar company.

Spiced tea and nuts, along with cheese straws, peppermint chocolate, and other yummy munchies, tide over empty tummies, while the merry buzz of dinner preparations continue in the kitchen. Children play a guessing game as they inspect the pile of presents—boxes of hopes and dreams all wrapped up with pretty satin ribbons and velvet bows.

The timer calls loudly, and Mother removes from the oven a mouthwatering masterpiece, a 24-pound turkey. Side dishes join the appetizing spread—all requested favorites such as corn soufflé and that family mealtime mainstay macaroni and cheese. The entire family gathers around. With clasped hands, they offer up a prayer of thankfulness for the blessings so abundant and this season that celebrates the greatest gift of all: love.

The aroma of cinnamon and citrus. The sound of jingling bells and sweetly sung carols. The feeling of Christmas, so tender and warm, fills our home with comfort and joy.

There is a reason we say, "Merry Christmas." It is because this season is filled so fully with merriment! With evergreen boughs joyfully bearing keepsake ornaments and handmade garlands, a magnificent tree proudly proclaims that this is indeed the most wonderful time of the year. White lights like miniature diamonds shimmer amid these verdant branches and wink as if they know the secrets inside the gifts below. Swags of greenery adorn the mantle, transforming it from a simple shelf to a showcase of seasonal treasures. And stockings of velvet and quilted satin hang expectantly at the hearth, awaiting the arrival of Father Christmas.

Beribboned ornaments suspended from the chandelier, sumptuous linens draping the dinner table, and the reflection of candlelight dancing in crystal stemware—each sparkling detail joins together in a divine display. Presented with the utmost grace and respect in a thoughtfully chosen place, a humble manger scene arranged on a bed of fresh greenery tells the story of long ago that brought forth the reason for this blessed and beloved season.

Tis the Season

Set the stage for St. Nick to make his infamous deliveries by decking your halls and walls, staircases and fireplaces with seasonal splendor. Fruit and feathers offer festive flair, especially when paired with beribboned badges of greenery. Embellished stockings complete the jolly setting, suspended in splendid anticipation of Santa's arrival.

Gifts & Goodies

Varied heights of silver pedestal servers, the tall and the small, pair with pillar candles to provide a lovely presentation for tasty tidbits. Candies, cookies, and cheese straws entice a hungry crowd, while a pile of pretty presents, wrapped in sumptuous fabrics, playfully piques curiosity.

Visions of Sugarplums

An angel statuary anchors an assemblage of red roses, lush greenery, and appetizing fruits and chocolates, turning the dining room buffet into quite a sweet sight. And as added delights, personalized plate decorations double as take-home ornaments that guests can treasure on their trees for years to come.

Menu

Hot Spiced Tea

Sage Cornbread

Cinnamon-Orange Spiced Nuts

Seasoned Nuts

Roasted Turkey with Herb Butter

Roasted Haricot Vert

Caramelized Sweet Potatoes and Pineapple

Cranberry Relish

Corn Soufflé

Eggnog Bread Pudding

Hot Spiced Tea

Entertaining Touches

Dress up the holiday meal with signature embellishments and garnishes. Add a clove-studded lemon slice to a steaming cup of spiced tea. Accent a tray of cornbread muffins with cheerful sprigs of cedar. Weave gossamer ribbons around serving pieces, interspersing the strands with bright blossoms. These entertaining extras only take a minute or two, but they bring a holly jolly measure of excitement to the holiday cheer.

Sage Cornbread

Sage Cornbread
Makes 12 servings

1¹/₂ cups self-rising cornmeal mix
1¹/₂ teaspoons dried sage
¹/₂ teaspoon poultry seasoning
1¹/₂ cups buttermilk
¹/₄ cup butter, melted
1 large egg, beaten

■ Preheat oven to 450°. In a medium bowl, combine cornmeal mix, sage, and poultry seasoning. Add buttermilk, butter, and egg; mix well.

■ Generously grease a 12-cup muffin pan with butter; place in oven to melt butter. Evenly spoon batter into cups; bake for 15 to 20 minutes, or until golden brown.

Hot Spiced Tea
Makes about 2¹/₂ quarts

8 cups water
1¹/₂ teaspoons whole allspice
1 teaspoon whole cloves
5 cinnamon sticks
2 family-size tea bags
1 cup sugar
1 cup fresh orange juice
³/₄ cup pineapple juice
¹/₃ cup fresh lemon juice

■ In a large saucepan or Dutch oven, combine water, allspice, cloves, and cinnamon sticks. Bring to a boil over medium-high heat. Add tea bags and reduce heat to low; simmer for 6 minutes.

■ Remove tea bags and add sugar, orange juice, pineapple juice, and lemon juice; simmer for 15 minutes. Remove spices and serve hot.

Cinnamon-Orange Spiced Nuts
Makes about 6 cups

2 cups whole almonds
2 cups pecan halves
2 cups walnuts
1 cup sugar
1¹/₂ teaspoons ground cinnamon
¹/₂ teaspoon ground cloves
¹/₄ teaspoon salt
2 egg whites
1 tablespoon grated orange zest
¹/₂ cup butter, melted

■ Preheat oven to 325°. Spread nuts on a baking sheet. Bake for 10 to 15 minutes, or until lightly toasted, stirring occasionally.

■ In a small bowl, combine sugar, cinnamon, cloves, and salt. In a separate bowl, beat egg

whites with an electric mixer at high speed until soft peaks form. Continue beating, gradually adding sugar mixture, until stiff peaks form. Stir in orange zest; stir in nuts to coat completely.
■ Line a baking sheet with aluminum foil. Evenly pour melted butter on baking sheet; spread nut mixture in pan. Bake, stirring every 10 minutes, for 20 to 25 minutes, or until nuts are brown and no butter remains in pan. Cool completely; store in an airtight container.

Seasoned Nuts
Makes 4 cups

2 (11.5 ounce) cans unsalted mixed nuts
2 tablespoons butter
2 tablespoons Worcestershire sauce
3¹/₂ teaspoons seasoned salt, divided
1 teaspoon garlic powder
¹/₄ teaspoon cayenne pepper
1 tablespoon Creole seasoning

■ Preheat oven to 300°. Line a baking sheet with aluminum foil; set aside.
■ In a small saucepan, melt butter over medium heat. Stir in Worcestershire sauce, 2 teaspoons seasoned salt, garlic powder, and cayenne pepper. Bring to a simmer, stirring constantly.
■ In a large bowl, toss mixed nuts with butter mixture to coat completely. Place nuts onto prepared baking sheet in an even layer. Bake for 20 to 25 minutes, stirring every 10 minutes. Sprinkle with remaining seasoned salt, stirring to mix well. Cool completely and sprinkle with Creole seasoning, stirring to coat; store in an airtight container.

RIGHT: A blend of spices with the kick of cayenne makes Seasoned Nuts the goody of choice for pre-dinner nibbling. The sugary sidekick to these salty snacks, Cinnamon-Orange Spiced Nuts offer another option for snacking. Just be sure to give your company fair warning about the size and scrumptiousness of the forthcoming meal so they'll save plenty of room for the highlight of the night: the Christmas Eve smorgasbord.

Seasoned Nuts
Cinnamon-Orange Spiced Nuts

Roasted Turkey with Herb Butter

Caramelized Sweet Potatoes and Pineapple

ABOVE: Roasted to tender perfection and basted with savory herb butter, this alternate take on traditional turkey is sure to be a favorite for years to come. Though many families already have a preferred recipe for sweet potatoes, pineapple and brown sugar take the taste from familiar to phenomenal.

Roasted Turkey with Herb Butter
Makes 12 to 14 servings

2 cups butter, softened
1/2 cup chopped fresh rosemary
1/2 cup chopped fresh thyme
2 tablespoons chopped fresh garlic
1 1/2 teaspoons salt
1 teaspoon ground black pepper
1 (20 to 24-pound) whole turkey, washed, giblets removed

■ Preheat oven to 325°. In a medium bowl, combine butter, rosemary, thyme, garlic, salt, and pepper. Place turkey, breast-side up, on a rack in a roasting pan; pat dry with paper towels.
■ Evenly rub butter mixture on turkey skin and inside turkey. Truss legs with butcher's twine. Cover with aluminum foil and bake for 4 hours.
■ Remove foil and continue baking 1 to 1 1/2 hours or until meat thermometer inserted into the thigh reaches 180°; baste occasionally with pan juices during last 1 to 1 1/2 hours. Remove pan from oven and let rest for 10 minutes.

Roasted Haricot Vert
Makes 10 to 12 servings

6 quarts water
1 tablespoon salt
3 pounds haricot vert, washed and trimmed
3 tablespoons fresh lemon juice
2 1/2 teaspoons garlic salt
1/4 teaspoon ground black pepper
1/4 cup olive oil

■ Preheat oven to 450°. Line a large roasting pan with aluminum foil; set aside.
■ In a large Dutch oven or stockpot, combine water and salt. Bring to a boil over medium-high heat. Add haricot vert and cook for 8 to 10 minutes, until just tender. Drain, rinse with cold water, and drain again.
■ In a large bowl, combine lemon juice, garlic salt, and pepper; whisk in olive oil until well blended. Add haricot vert and toss to coat completely; place in prepared pan. Bake for 25 to 30 minutes, stirring every 10 minutes.

Caramelized Sweet Potatoes and Pineapple
Makes 10 to 12 servings

1/2 cup butter
1 cup firmly packed dark brown sugar
2 tablespoons water
2 teaspoons ground cinnamon
1/2 teaspoon ground ginger
1/2 teaspoon salt
5 large sweet potatoes, peeled
1 pineapple, peeled and cored

■ Preheat oven to 400°. In a medium saucepan, melt butter over medium heat. Add brown sugar, water, cinnamon, ginger, and salt. Bring to a simmer, stirring constantly, until sugar has dissolved.
■ Cut sweet potatoes into 1/4-inch thick slices; set aside. Cut pineapple into 1/2-inch thick slices; cut pineapple slices into fourths. In a large bowl, combine sweet potatoes and pineapple. Add butter mixture and gently toss to coat well. Arrange sweet potatoes and pineapple in a large roasting pan and cover tightly with aluminum foil; bake for 1 hour.
■ Preheat oven to 475°. Remove foil from pan and baste with syrup from potatoes. Bake in upper third of oven, basting periodically, for 20 to 25 minutes until syrup thickens and potatoes caramelize.
■ Serve immediately, or keep warm in a low-degree oven up to 30 minutes. Baste just before serving.

Cranberry Relish
Makes about 5 1/2 cups

5 medium Granny Smith apples, cored and diced
2 (6-ounce) packages dried cranberries
2 cups cranberry-apple juice drink
3/4 cup sugar
1/2 cup fresh orange juice
1 tablespoon orange zest

■ In a large saucepan or Dutch oven, combine all ingredients over medium-high heat. Bring mixture to a boil, then reduce heat. Simmer for 15 to 20 minutes, stirring occasionally, until apples are tender.

Roasted Haricot Vert
Cranberry Relish

Corn Soufflé

Soufflé Illusion

There's a bit of deception surrounding the delectable dish known as corn soufflé. It appears as if the cook has toiled for hours to make this fluffy and rich offering when in fact, it is fairly easy to make. You may use fresh corn, but frozen works equally well and requires less fuss. The key to the soufflé's fluffiness lies in adding whipped egg whites just before baking. There is no need to let guests in on the illusion—just enjoy the compliments. For best results, plan accordingly so that the soufflé is the last dish out of the oven before serving.

Corn Soufflé
Makes 10 to 12 servings

3 tablespoons butter, divided
2 tablespoons all-purpose flour
1 cup heavy whipping cream
2 tablespoons sugar
1 teaspoon salt
1/4 teaspoon ground white pepper
4 cups frozen white creamed corn, thawed
5 large eggs, separated

■ Preheat oven to 325°. Grease a 2½-quart soufflé dish with 1 tablespoon butter; set aside.
■ In a heavy-bottomed Dutch oven, melt 2 tablespoons butter over medium heat. Add flour and cook for 2 minutes, whisking constantly. Gradually add cream and bring to a simmer, whisking constantly. Add sugar, salt, and white pepper. Add corn and simmer for 1 minute. Whisking constantly, gradually add lightly beaten egg yolks and cook for 3 minutes, until mixture begins to thicken. Remove from heat and cool for 5 minutes.
■ In a large mixing bowl, beat egg whites at high speed with an electric mixer, beating until stiff peaks form. Gently fold egg whites into corn mixture. Pour into prepared soufflé dish placed on a baking sheet, and bake for 45 to 50 minutes on bottom rack of oven.

Eggnog Bread Pudding
Makes 10 to 12 servings

1 (16-ounce) loaf Hawaiian sweet bread, crust removed
1/2 cup butter, melted
2 cups milk
2 cups heavy whipping cream
1 cup sugar
1 teaspoon vanilla extract
3 tablespoons brandy
1/8 teaspoon salt
1 teaspoon ground nutmeg
8 large eggs
1 recipe Vanilla Rum Sauce (recipe follows)

■ Preheat oven to 325°.
■ Cut bread into 1-inch cubes; place in a large mixing bowl. Toss bread with melted butter; set aside. In a large saucepan, combine milk, cream, sugar, vanilla, brandy, salt, and nutmeg. Bring to a simmer over medium heat, stirring constantly, until sugar dissolves.
■ Whisk eggs until smooth. Slowly add hot milk mixture to eggs, whisking constantly. Pour custard mixture over bread; let stand for 10 minutes.
■ Pour mixture into a 13x9x2-inch baking dish and place in another larger pan. Pour enough hot water into larger pan to reach halfway up sides of baking dish.
■ Bake for 1 hour, or until the custard is set and the bread is golden brown. Loosely cover with foil halfway through baking time to prevent over-browning. Serve warm with Vanilla Rum Sauce.

Vanilla Rum Sauce:
Makes 1¾ cups

1/2 cup firmly packed light brown sugar
2 teaspoons cornstarch
1 cup heavy whipping cream
2 tablespoons light rum
1/2 cup butter, cut into pieces
1 teaspoon vanilla extract

■ In a medium saucepan, stir together sugar and cornstarch. Gradually add cream, stirring until smooth. Bring to a simmer over medium heat, stirring constantly. Add rum and simmer for 5 minutes, stirring constantly. Gradually add butter and stir until melted.
■ Remove from heat and stir in vanilla. Serve warm. Store sauce in refrigerator for up to 1 week.

Eggnog Bread Pudding

Credits & Acknowledgements

This book is the result of many talented hands and creative minds working together. The tremendous efforts of these individuals, along with their dedication to excellence, are reflected in the pages of **The Entertaining Touch**, *and with a grateful heart, I would like to extend sincere appreciation with these acknowledgements:*

To Phyllis Hoffman, publisher and president of Hoffman Media, who possessed the prowess and vision to pursue an entertaining book that would embody the graciousness and hospitality illustrated in *Southern Lady*, and who enabled us to use our creativity to translate that vision into a tangible collection of entertaining inspiration.

To Yukie McLean, style director and creative genius, who brought to life the ideas and themes of the majority of the parties; who did whatever was necessary—including braving the rain, shivering in the cold, and enduring the summer sun—to achieve just the right look and setting.

To Jordan Marxer, art director, who tirelessly worked with constant creative energy and infallible determination to transform an immense collection of prose and photographs into a masterful feast for the eyes.

To Rebecca Touliatos, test kitchen director, who added incredible inspiration and organization to this project, and who devoted countless hours to the remarkable recipes featured in the parties.

To Aimee Bishop, food editor, who adopted this project as a labor of love and committed an immeasurable amount of time and energy to ensure its completion; who brought to the table not only picture-perfect, innovative, and delicious dishes, but also creativity, laughter, and encouragement.

To Mac Jamieson, creative director, who captured the essence of entertaining with the lens of a camera; whose direction, wisdom, and encouragement helped guide the project from start to finish.

To Marcy Black and Arden Ward, photographers, who each lent their respective brilliance and talents to various parties; who, amid battling unpredictable weather conditions and marathon photo shoots, remained steadfast in providing exceedingly beautiful images.

To Delisa McDaniel, color technician, who worked her inexplicably lovely magic on each and every image to ensure the highest possible quality of visual appeal, and who invested much time and effort to see that standard exhibited throughout the book.

To Karen Dauphin and Lauren Rippey, writers and editorial contributors, who both rose to the occasion no matter the situation; who lent their individual talents and skills to the project, along with unfailing support and creative inspiration; who, with unparalleled grace and charm, helped shape the content that forms the heart and soul of this project.

To Ann Dorer, copy editor and epitome of a Southern lady, who in addition to inspiring excellence and beauty, helped shape the text with her expert eye and aptitude for eloquence.

To Greg Baugh, production manager, who provided organization and motivation throughout the project; who helped guide and schedule along the way to ensure quality and completion.

To the stylists and chefs who contributed their talents and time to this project; to the homeowners who opened their hearts and homes for location photo shoots; to those at shops and stores who offered countless props and services; to our families and friends who gave throughout this project and continue to give their love and support; to my Lord and Savior—thank you.

The Entertaining Essentials
Illustrations by Breanne Jackson
Special Thanks to Lindsay Keith, Truax & Co., and Table Matters

The Entertaining Extras
Special Thanks to Karissa Brown and Ann Dorer

Painting Party: Colorful Companionship
Recipe Development and Food Styling by Aimee Bishop
Photography by Marcy Black
Invitations by Brandi K. Etheredge of Brandi K. Etheredge Designs
Painting Techniques and Artistry by Itsuko McKinney
Location provided by Caterina Meadows

Porch Party: The Spice of Life
Recipe Development and Food Styling by Aimee Bishop
Photography by Arden Ward and Marcy Black
Invitations by Lindsay Keith
Location provided by Glynne Lassiter

Evening Elegance: The Black & White Party
Recipe Development and Food Styling by Aimee Bishop, Chocolate Sushi Developed and Styled by Morgan Cobern
Photography by Mac Jamieson
Floral Designs by Dorothy McDaniel's Flower Market
Invitations and Menu by Lauren Goessling of Lauren Goessling Designs
Location provided by Sara Rast
Special Thanks to Waterford and Godiva

Wine & Dine: Taste of Tuscany
Recipe Development and Food Styling by Aimee Bishop
Photography by Mac Jamieson
Floral Desgins by Dorothy McDaniel's Flower Market
Invitations by Brandi K. Etheredge of Brandi K. Etheredge Designs
Location provided by Steve and Becky Boner
Special Thanks to Thomas C. LaBoone of the Village Wine Market and to Vietri

Flower Swap: For the Garden Club
Styling by Carol Riley of Lillie's
Recipe Development and Food Styling by Aimee Bishop
Photography by Mac Jamieson
Invitations by Lauren Goessling of Lauren Goessling Designs
Location provided by Lauren Welden

Fairytale Birthday: Of Wings & Whimsy
Recipe Development and Food Styling by Rebecca Touliatos
Photography by Arden Ward
Floral Designs by Dorothy McDaniel's Flower Market
Location provided by Barbara Randall
Special Thanks to Mara Joy Luker of Lily Anna for Girls and to Vietri

Silver Settings: Luncheon For the Ladies
Recipe Development and Food Styling by Aimee Bishop
Photography by Mac Jamieson
Floral Designs by Dorothy McDaniel's Flower Market
Location provided by Beth Simpson

Sea & Shore: Best of the Beach
Recipe Development and Food Styling by Aimee Bishop
Photography by Arden Ward
Invitations by Brandi K. Etheredge of Brandi K. Etheredge Designs
Location provided by Southern Resorts
Special Thanks to Tracy Louthain and the Beaches of South Walton

Well Served: The Courtside Soiree
Recipe Development and Food Styling by Aimee Bishop
Photography by Marcy Black
Invitations by Shane and Brandi K. Etheredge of Brandi K. Etheredge Designs
Location provided by Cherry Starr

Open House: Warm Welcomes
Recipe Development and Food Styling by Aimee Bishop

Photography by Mac Jamieson
Location provided by Becky Jones

Poolside Grill: For the Bride & Groom
Recipe Development and Food Styling by Criss Smiley
Photography by Marcy Black and Mac Jamieson
Invitations by Brandi K. Etheredge of Brandi K. Etheredge Designs
Location provided by Becky Jones

On the Lawn: Golden Afternoon
Recipe Development and Food Styling by Aimee Bishop
Photography by Mac Jamieson and Marcy Black
Invitations by Brandi K. Etheredge of Brandi K. Etheredge Designs
Location provided by Aldridge Gardens

Dinner for Two: Candlelight Sonata
Styling by Harriet H. Luce of Fetes en Fleur
Recipe Development and Food Styling by Chef Antony Osborne and Chef Robby Melvin of Culinard, The Culinary Institute of Virginia College
Photography by Arden Ward
Location provided by Jane Hoke
Special Thanks to Nicholas Hartmann of Nicholas Hartmann Ice by Design

Of Faith & Love: White Bible Ceremony
Recipe Development by Rebecca Touliatos and Criss Smiley, Food Styling by Criss Smiley
Photography by Mac Jamieson
Location provided by Kimeran Stevens
Special Thanks to Lynn Terry

Gathered Together: Home for the Holidays
Styling by Melanie Hughes
Recipe Development and Food Styling by Aimee Bishop
Photography by Marcy Black and Mac Jamieson
Invitations by Brandi K. Etheredge of Brandi K. Etheredge Designs
Location provided by Melanie Hughes
Special thanks to Bill Aroosian of Habitation

For information about companies listed, please see DIRECTORY OF COMPANIES on page 189.

Resources & Directory of Companies

To purchase items featured in this book, please refer to the information below. If an item is not listed, it is privately owned and not available for purchase. To contact the manufacturers and retail stores referenced below, see Directory of Companies.

Entertaining Essentials

Pages 8-13: Plates, silver, and crystal from Truax & Co.
Pages 14-15: China, crystal, and linens from Table Matters. Flatware from Bromberg's.
Pages 16-19: See respective parties for information.

Entertaining Extras

Page 24: Top Left: Blue napkin and black, white, and green dinnerware from Lamb's Ears, Ltd.
Page 25: Miniature grapevine wreath from Hobby Lobby.
Page 26: Silver charger, dinnerware, and silverware from Truax & Co. White monogrammed napkin from Martha Lauren Antique Linens & Accessories.
Page 27: Black dinnerware and silverware from Truax & Co. Floral-patterned napkin from Table Matters.
Pages 28-29: Aqua-banded china from Truax & Co. Taupe napkin from Table Matters.
Page 30: Gold-rimmed china from Truax & Co. Yellow-striped napkin from Table Matters.
Page 31: Patterned gold-rimmed china from Truax & Co. Vintage napkin from Martha Lauren Antique Linens & Accessories.
Page 32: Red and gold china from Truax & Co.
Page 33: Blue-patterned china and silverware from Truax & Co. Scalloped napkin from Martha Lauren Antique Linens & Accessories.

Painting Party: Colorful Companionship

Page 36: Paint cans from Royal Paints, Inc.
Page 37: Paint swatches from Home Depot.
Pages 38-39: Paint cans and brushes from Royal Paints, Inc. Colored napkins and green plates from Lamb's Ears, Ltd.
Page 39: Stepladder bookcase and decorative jugs from Met Fabrics. Serving tray from Mulberry Heights.
Page 40: Wall art and lamps from Met Fabrics. Fabric upholstery from Pate Meadows Designs. Monogrammed pillows from Grafix South. Folding animal-print tray from Cabbages & Kings.
Page 42: Yellow casserole dish from Christine's. Red dip bowl from Lamb's Ears, Ltd.
Page 43: Brown and white flower pots from Mulberry Heights Antiques. Pink serving bowl from Lamb's Ears, Ltd.
Page 44: Green serving platter from Lamb's Ears, Ltd.

Porch Party: The Spice of Life

Page 46: Serving platter, flower vases, and wreath from Harmony Landing.
Pages 48-49: Rustic-colored plates, bowls, and napkins from Harmony Landing.
Page 50: Large serving bowls from Harmony Landing.
Page 51: Glasses from Pottery Barn.
Page 54: Mugs and glasses from Harmony Landing

Evening Elegance: The Black & White Party

Page 56: Ballet ribbon china, crystal, and stemware from Waterford. Black napkins and chargers from Pier 1 Imports. Black and white striped napkin rings from Table Matters. White tablecloth from Martha Lauren Antique Linens & Accessories. Candle holders from Table Matters, Christine's, and Lamb's Ears, Ltd.
Page 60: Truffles from Godiva. Ornament ball from Lamb's Ears, Ltd. Knife rest from Martha Lauren Antique Linens & Accessories.
Pages 62-63: Tuxedos from Mr. Burch Formal Wear. Dresses from White House/Black Market, Jessica McClintock, Inc., and Gus Mayer.
Page 63: Candelabras from Tricia's Treasures. Black and white candleholders from Habitation.
Page 64: Cocktail glasses from Table Matters.

Wine & Dine: Taste of Tuscany

Page 68: Marble-top iron stand from Table Matters. Dinnerware and serving platters from Vietri. Various wines from Village Wine Market. Antique wicker wine jugs from Arceneaux Gallery. Cloth napkins from Christine's.
Page 70: Copper bowl from Table Matters.
Page 72: Platter from Vietri.
Page 74: Stopper from Table Matters. White napkin from Williams Sonoma.

Flower Swap: For the Garden Club

Page 76: Plates and cups from McCarty's Pottery. Bowls from Peter's Pottery.
Page 79: Plants and seedlings from Collier's Nursery. Green and white ribbon from Smith's Variety.
Pages 80-81: Ceramic lambs from Peter's Pottery.
Page 85: Martini glasses from Table Matters.

Fairytale Birthday: Of Wings & Whimsy

Page 86: Leotards, wings, and tutus from Lily Anna for Girls. Flower wreaths from Dorothy McDaniel's Flower Market.
Page 89: Tiered butterfly cake from Edgar's Bakery. Butterfly dishes from Vietri.
Page 91: Flower vases and tablecloth from Homewood Florist.

Silver Settings: Luncheon for the Ladies

Pages 96: Silver chargers from Anthropologie.
Note: All china and silver is privately owned.

Sea & Shore: Best of the Beach

Page 104: Crab napkin ring from Table Matters. Blue and white napkins and blue flatware from Harmony Landing. Shells from J. Marshall Sims Collection. Shell-embellished chargers, blue and white plates, and candle holders from Pottery Barn. Stemware from Pier 1 Imports.
Page 110: Pearlized charger from Magnolia House.
Page 113: Silver serving platter from Flora.

Well Served: Courtside Soiree

Page 114: Flower vase from Harmony Landing. Printed napkins, chargers, and plates from Anthropologie. Glasses from Harmony Landing.
Page 116: Long crystal stemware from Cabbages & Kings.
Page 117: Monogrammed towels from The Blue Willow.
Pages 118-119: Tiered serving tray from Summerhill, Ltd. Glass flower vases from Pottery Barn.

Open House: Warm Welcomes

Pages 124-133: *Note: All decorative items are privately owned.*

Poolside Grill: For the Bride & Groom

Page 134: Colored dinnerware and glasses from Pottery Barn.
Page 136-137: Glass hurricane containers (shown poolside) from Dorothy McDaniel's Flower Market.

Page 139: Green placemats, blue napkins, and stemware from Pottery Barn.

Page 140: Colored dinnerware from Pottery Barn. Glass jars of varying heights from Habitation.

Page 142: Tiered server from Harmony Landing.

On the Lawn: Golden Afternoon

Pages 150-151: Large flower container from Sweet Peas Garden Shop. Dessert goblets and juice pitchers from Cabbages & Kings. Serving platter and cake stands from Flora.

Dinner for Two: Candlelight Sonata

Page 156: Violin and sheet music from Art's Music Shop, Inc.

Page 157: Embossed ivory stationery, floral velum, and sheet music scrapbook paper from A.C. Moore.

Page 159: Instruments from Art's Music Shop, Inc. Gold-rimmed dinnerware, glassware, linens, placemats, and salt and pepper shakers from Table Matters.

Page 160: Floral-patterned plate from Table Matters.

Page 163: Ice sculpture from Nicholas Hartmann Ice by Design.

Of Faith & Love: White Bible Ceremony

Page 166: White Bible from Books-A-Million.

Page 168: Handkerchief from Martha Lauren Antique Linens & Accessories.

Page 169: Tussie-mussie from Dorothy McDaniel's Flower Market.

Gathered Together: Home for the Holidays

Page 174: Christmas balls, bird nests, and twigs from Greenbrier Furniture, Inc.

Page 175: Gold charger, gold ball, crystal salt and pepper shakers from Table Matters.

Page 176: Red vases from Greenbrier Furniture, Inc.

Page 177: Salt and pepper shakers from Table Matters. China and silverware from Bromberg's. Yellow cake stand from Greenbrier Furniture, Inc. Glassware from Table Matters.

Page 178: Angel statuary from Lamb's Ears, Ltd.

Page 181: Silver bowls and serving pieces from Tricia's Trea-

---

DIRECTORY OF COMPANIES

A.C. Moore, www.acmoore.com.

Anthropologie, www.anthropologie.com.

Arceneaux Gallery, 2880 Old Rocky Ridge Road, Suite 100, Birmingham, AL 35243; 205-824-5800.

Art's Music Shop, Inc., 4647 Highway 280, Birmingham, AL 35242; 205-995-8376.

Beaches of South Walton, www.beachesofsouthwalton.com.

The Blue Willow, 3930 Crosshaven Drive, Birmingham, AL 35243; 205-968-0909.

Books-A-Million, www.booksamillion.com.

Brandi K. Etheredge Designs, bke.design@yahoo.com.

Bromberg's, www.brombergs.com.

Cabbages & Kings, 620 27th Street South, Birmingham, AL 35233; 205-731-9952.

Christine's, 2822 Petticoat Lane, Mountain Brook, AL 35223; 205-871-8297.

Collier's Nursery, 2904 Old Rocky Ridge Road, Birmingham, AL 35243; 205-822-3133.

Culinard, The Culinary Institute of Virginia College, www.culinard.com.

Dorothy McDaniel's Flower Market, 2560 18th Street South, Birmingham, AL 35209; 205-871-0092.

Edgar's Bakery, 499 Southgate Drive, Pelham, AL 35124; 205-987-8551.

Fetes en Fleur, A Division of Hawkins-Israel III Interiors, 706-296-1360.

Flora, 1911 Oxmoor Road, Homewood, AL 35209; 205-871-4004.

Godiva, www.godiva.com.

Grafix South, 1912 2nd Avenue North, Bessemer, AL 35020; 205-426-6004.

Greenbrier Furniture, Inc., 1493 Montgomery Highway, Birmingham, AL 35216; 205-822-7456.

Gus Mayer, 604 Brookwood Village, Birmingham, AL 35209; 205-870-3300.

Habitation, 936 Oxmoor Road, Homewood, AL 35209; 205-879-5558.

Harmony Landing, 2925 18th Street South, Homewood, AL 35209; 205-871-0585.

Hobby Lobby, www.hobbylobby.com.

Home Depot, www.homedepot.com.

Homewood Florist, 940 Oxmoor Road, Homewood, AL 35209; 205-870-8809.

Itsuko McKinney, 5941 South Crest Road, Birmingham, AL 35213; 205-592-3669.

Jessica McClintock, Inc., www.jessicamcclintock.com.

J. Marshall Sims Collection, Interiors at Pepper Place, 2817 2nd Avenue South, Birmingham, AL 35233; 205-323-2817.

Lamb's Ears, Ltd., 3138 Cahaba Heights Road, Birmingham, AL 35243; 205-969-3138.

Lauren Goessling Designs, www.laurengoesslingdesigns.com.

Lillie's, 2713 Millbrook Road, Birmingham, AL 35243, 205-296-3457.

Lily Anna for Girls, www.lilyannaforgirls.com; 801-485-1890.

Martha Lauren Antique Linens & Accessories, 2417 Canterbury Road, Mountain Brook, AL 35223; 205-871-2283.

McCarty's Pottery, 101 Saint Mary Street, Merigold, MS 38759; 662-748-2293.

Met Fabrics, 3005 3rd Avenue South, Birmingham, AL 35233; 205-322-5497.

Mr. Burch Formal Wear, www.mrburchformalwear.com.

Mulberry Heights Antiques, 2419 Canterbury Road, Mountain Brook, AL 35223; 205-870-1300.

Magnolia House, 2 Magnolia Street, Grayton Beach, FL 32459; 888-272-3250.

Nicholas Hartmann Ice by Design, 3600 Wyngate Lane, Birmingham, AL 35242; 205-980-8610.

Pate Meadows Designs, 1904 2nd Avenue North, Bessemer, AL 35020; 205-424-1770.

Peter's Pottery, 301 Fortune Avenue, Mound Bayou, MS 38762; 662-741-2283.

Pier 1 Imports, www.pier1.com.

Pottery Barn, www.potterybarn.com.

Royal Paints, Inc., 7960 Crestwood Boulevard, Irondale, AL 35210; 205-956-9024.

Smith's Variety, 2715 Culver Road, Mountain Brook, AL 35223; 205-871-0841.

Southern Resorts, www.southernresorts.com.

Summerhill, Ltd., 2901 18th Street South, Homewood, AL 35209; 205-871-2902.

Sweet Peas Garden Shop, 2829 Linden Avenue, Homewood, AL 35209; 205-879-3839.

Table Matters, 2402 Montevallo Road, Mountain Brook, AL 35223; 205-879-0125.

Tricia's Treasures, 2700 19th Place South, Homewood, AL 35209; 205-871-9779.

Truax & Co., 125 Broad Street, Selma, AL 36701; 334-874-9600.

Vietri, www.vietri.com.

Village Wine Market, 2020 Cahaba Road, Birmingham, AL 35223; 205-879-5240.

Waterford, www.waterford.com.

White House/Black Market, www.whiteandblack.com.

Williams Sonoma, www.williams-sonoma.com.

Recipe Index